COME LEARN
WITH ME

COME LEARN WITH ME

By Ramona Watts and LaVona B. Dickinson

Fearon Teacher Aids
Belmont, California

Illustrated by: Duane Bibby

ISBN 0-8224-1377-9

Printed in the United States of America

1.9 8 7 6 5 4 3 2 1

Contents

Introduction

This book contains 21 lesson plans with reproducible activity pages for preschool children. Each lesson consists of five parts: Opening Activities, Listen and Learn, Storytime, Activities, and Closing.

Opening Activities

begin with a patriotic, flag-waving march followed by the Pledge of Allegiance. Attendance is taken with the use of a name-recognition chart, followed by a look at the weather, the calendar, and some favorite finger-plays. Complete instructions for making all charts and materials for these activities are given at the beginning of the book.

Listen and Learn

provides information and discussion material centered on the day's theme. Use it to generate enthusiasm and impart knowledge. Use your own creativity, and add suitable material to meet the needs of your students.

Be positive and encouraging with children. **Give praise continually,** and don't expect children to do more than they are able. If they don't know answers, tell them. These lessons are designed not to be a test of knowledge, but to provide learning experience. Encourage participation and praise any efforts the children make.

Storytime

suggests stories to be read to children that are published in a separate book as a supplement to the *Come Learn With Me* curriculum, entitled *Storytime Learning*. Alternate books on a similar theme could also be used.

Hints for effective storytelling:

1. Practice reading the story in advance, and be prepared to read smoothly and with expression.

2. Before reading the story, give children a purpose for listening. Ask them to listen or look for something specific, and then be sure to ask them about it at the end of the story.

3. If children are very young, tell the story to them rather than read it, and point to the pictures. Use your judgment based on the attention span of your children.

4. Help children develop an eye for detail by pointing out specific details in pictures.

5. Follow up with questions to give children practice recalling details.

Activities

include crafts, songs, and dramatic play to provide active learning opportunities. Allow children the freedom to express themselves in their own unique way.

When children are making crafts, be careful not to "fix" their projects. The projects are intended to provide opportunities for small muscle and eye-hand coordination. The finished product is not as important as the process.

Children are not expected to be able to trace or cut. If a project requires this, it must be done ahead of time.

Closing

is a review of the day's activities. It can vary in length, depending on time and the interest of the children.

Each lesson was carefully designed to help teachers, caregivers, and mothers provide children with a stimulating learning environment. Be creative, laugh, enjoy yourself, and the children will "catch" your enthusiasm for learning.

Instructions for Making Weather Chart

Materials:
- two posterboard halves (22" x 14")
- two 18" x 18" pieces of posterboard for stands
- "Weather Children"
- weather symbols and clothes
- marking pens
- clear contact paper
- masking tape
- glue

Weather Chart

1. After coloring and cutting out weather children, glue them on the bottom of one of the posterboards, and add the title "Weather Chart" at the top (figure A).

2. Cover both posterboards with clear contact paper.

3. After weather symbols and clothes are colored, cover both sides with clear contact paper. Cut them out.

4. Roll a small piece of masking tape, and stick it to the back of all symbols and clothes. The tape remains sticky for quite a while and will allow you to take the items off and restick them again.

Each day when you do the weather chart with the children, allow them to choose the appropriate clothes and symbols off the board to stick on the weather chart (figure B).

Stand

1. Fold 18" x 18" posterboard in half.

2. Measure and draw cutting lines (figure C).

3. Cut. Open and use as a stand for any chart (figure B).

Weather Diagrams

(figure A)

(figure B)

(figure C)

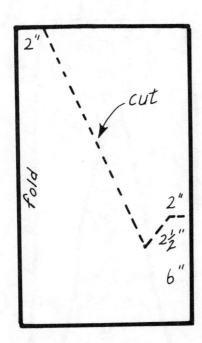

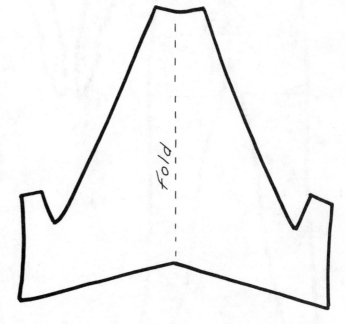

Weather Children

Color, cut out, and glue on weather chart.

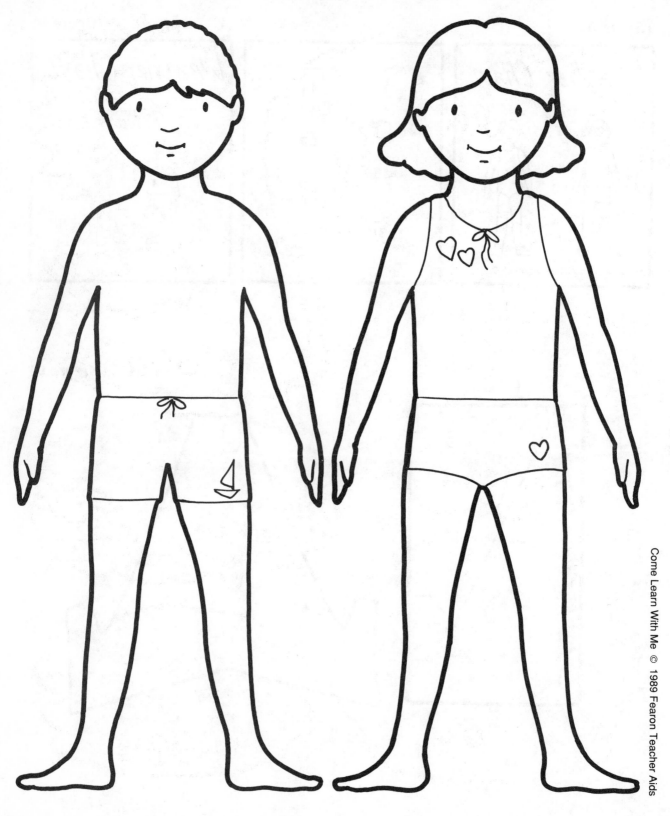

Come Learn With Me © 1989 Fearon Teacher Aids

Weather Symbols

Color, cut out, and cover with clear contact paper.

11

Clothes

Color, cut out, and cover with clear contact paper.

Come Learn With Me © 1989 Fearon Teacher Aids

Clothes

Color, cut out, and cover with clear contact paper.

Instructions for Making Calendar

Materials:
- half sheet of posterboard (22" x 14")
- 18" x 18" piece of posterboard for stand
- yardstick
- calendar decorations on pages 15–26
- glue, scissors, marking pens, pencil

figure A

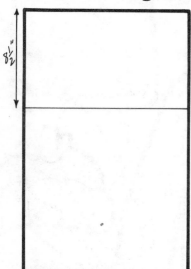

1. Lay the posterboard vertically in front of you. Measure down 8 1/2" from the top, and draw a horizontal line (figure A).

2. Measure and draw six vertical lines 2" apart in the lower portion of the calendar (figure B).

3. Measure and draw five horizontal lines 2 1/2" apart in the lower portion of the calendar, beginning at the bottom (figure C).

4. This will leave a 1" strip at the top of the lined grid. Write the names of the days of the week in those spaces (figure D).

5. Cover with clear contact paper.

6. Make a folding stand to hold the calendar. (See instructions under weather chart).

7. Color, cover with clear contact paper, and cut out decorations and daily number emblems.

figure B

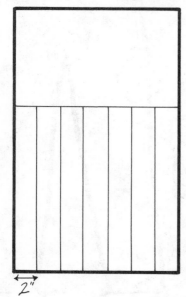

figure C

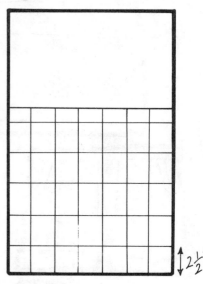

figure D

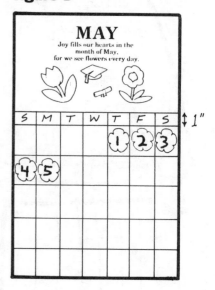

JANUARY

January brings lots of fun, for a new year has begun.

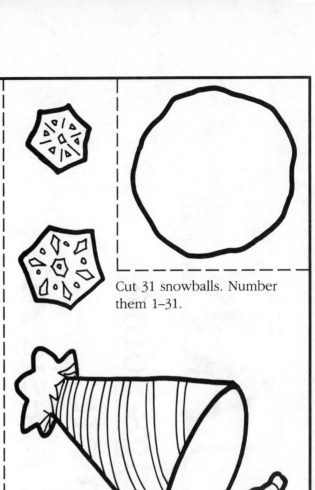

Cut 31 snowballs. Number them 1–31.

FEBRUARY

February brings some
great events:
Valentines and presidents!

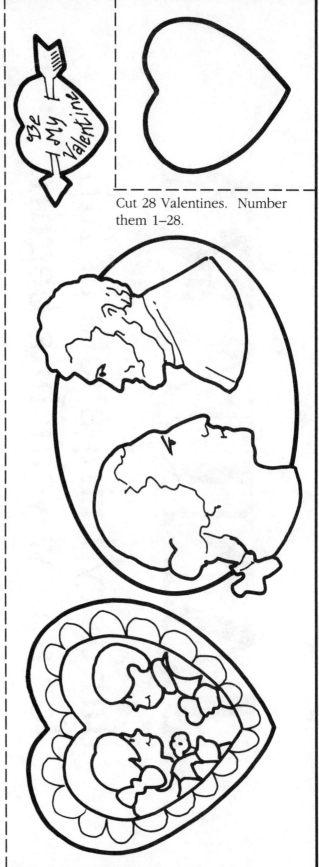

Cut 28 Valentines. Number
them 1–28.

MARCH

The March winds blow high,
They toss our kites into the sky.

Cut 31 kites. Number them 1–31.

APRIL

In April, Spring is in the air. Buds and green leaves are everywhere.

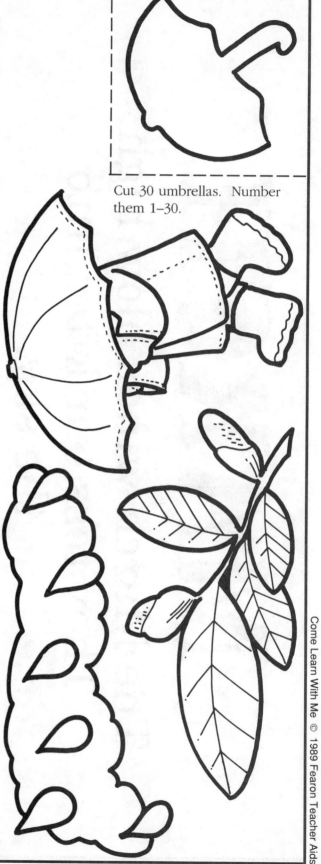

Cut 30 umbrellas. Number them 1–30.

Come Learn With Me © 1989 Fearon Teacher Aids

MAY

Joy fills our hearts in the month of May, for we see flowers every day.

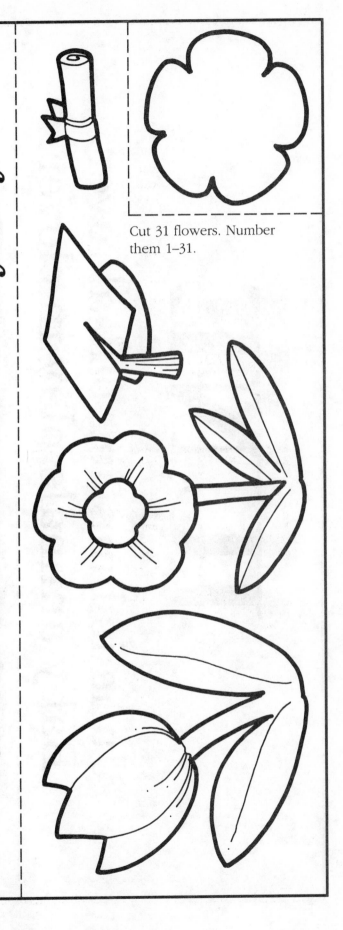

Cut 31 flowers. Number them 1–31.

JUNE

June is bursting out all over.
Baby animals play in clover.

Cut 30 butterflies. Number
them 1–30.

CERTIFICATE
Worlds' Best Dad!

Come Learn With Me © 1989 Fearon Teacher Aids

JULY

Freedom we gained on the "4th of July."

Our hopes and dreams can soar to the sky.

Cut 31 stars. Number them 1–31.

AUGUST

August brings summer fun, playing and swimming in the sun.

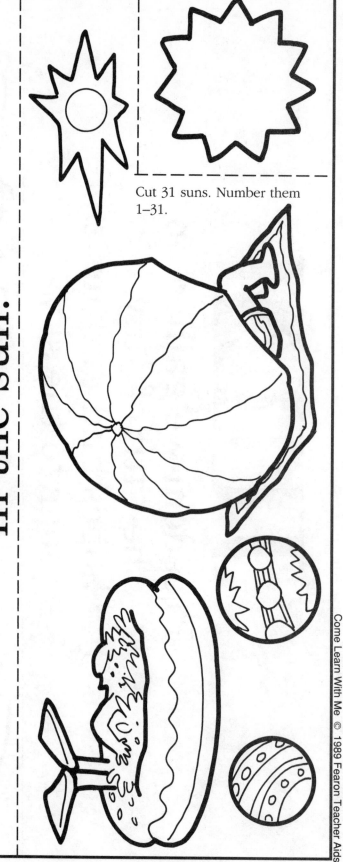

Cut 31 suns. Number them 1–31.

SEPTEMBER

If it's school you will pursue,
September is the month
for you.

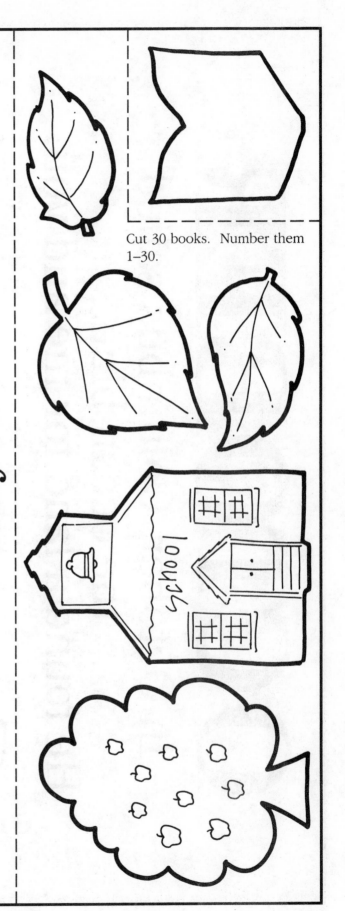

Cut 30 books. Number them 1–30.

OCTOBER

In October, Columbus sailed the ocean blue.

He found a land for me and you.

Cut 31 Jack-o-lanterns.
Number them 1–31.

Come Learn With Me © 1989 Fearon Teacher Aids

NOVEMBER

Thanksgiving is in November.
Turkeys and pies we all remember!

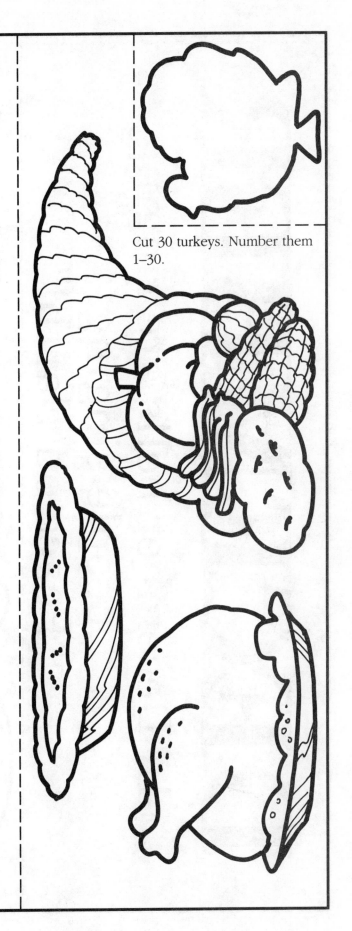

Cut 30 turkeys. Number them 1–30.

DECEMBER

In December bells are ringing,
people singing,
"Peace on Earth!"

Cut 31 bells. Number them 1–31.

Instructions for Making Name Chart

Materials:
- "Home" and "School" strips
- boy and girl figures (one for each boy and girl)
- tape
- marking pens
- two posterboards (8 1/2" x__ depending on number of children)*
- two pieces of construction paper (4" x__ same length as posterboard)
- clear contact paper
- stapler

*You will need approximately 3" per child, so if the chart is for three children, the posterboard should be 8 1/2" x 9". If the chart is for five children, the posterboard should be 8 1/2" x 15".

figure A

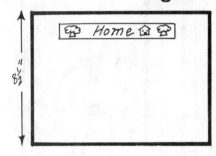

1. Color the "Home" strip and glue it on the top of the posterboard (figure A).

2. Lay construction paper over bottom portion of posterboard to make the pockets. Tape securely around the edges, and staple to make 3" pockets (figure B).

figure B

tape edges

3. Write each child's name on one pocket of the name chart (figure C).

4. Repeat each of the above three steps to make the "School" pocket chart.

5. Write each child's name at the top of the boy or girl (figure D). Allow children to color their own figures. Then cover with clear contact paper.

6. During the "Name Time" of each day's opening activities, put figures in pockets (figure E).

7. If your charts are not too large, you can connect them with tape and fold them together for easy storage (figure F).

figure C

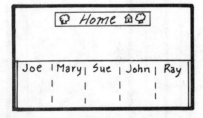

figure D

figure E

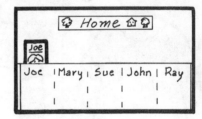

figure F

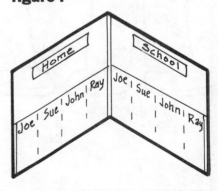

Name Chart

(strips and figures)

Instructions for Making Fingerplay Chart

Materials:
- one fingerplay chart from pages 31-37 reproduced on colorful construction paper
- fingerplay figure pattern from page 30 to match chart
- clear contact paper
- tape

1. Cover chart with clear contact paper. (For a sturdier chart, mount it on cardboard.)

2. Reproduce one fingerplay figure for each fingerplay you are putting on the chart. Put a number on the back of each figure.

3. On a master list, write what fingerplay corresponds to each number.

4. Cover all figures with contact paper, and use tape to stick them to the chart.

Make the fingerplay charts as attractive and colorful as you like. If, for example, you are using the gumball chart, make each gumball a different color. This will also help children with color-recognition skills.

Use fingerplays during opening activities, to get the "wiggles" out before storytime, or during the closing moments of the day.

Allow children to take a figure off the chart. Look up the number on the corresponding master list, and do that fingerplay together with the children.

Here's a helpful hint if you have trouble remembering whom you have chosen to pick a fingerplay and who has not yet had a turn. Make a similar chart and put children's names on the figures. When you choose a child to be a helper in some way, take that child's name off the chart. When all the names are gone and everyone has had a turn, you can begin again. Put names that have been chosen in an envelope attached to the back of the chart.

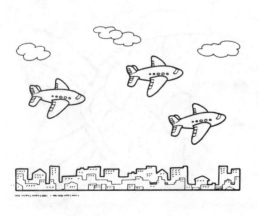

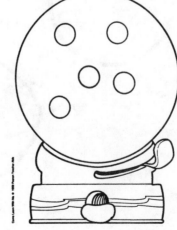

Fingerplay Figures

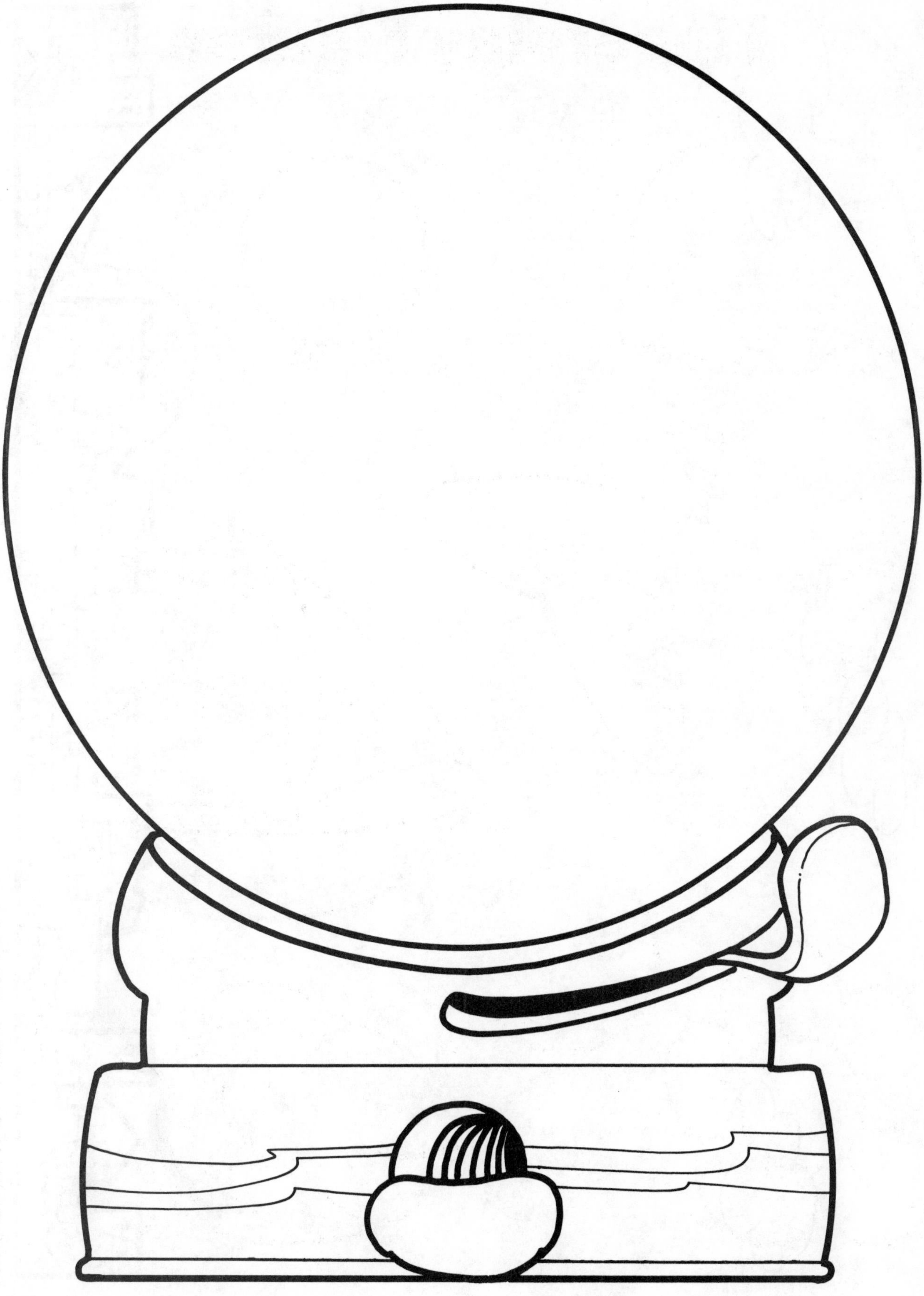

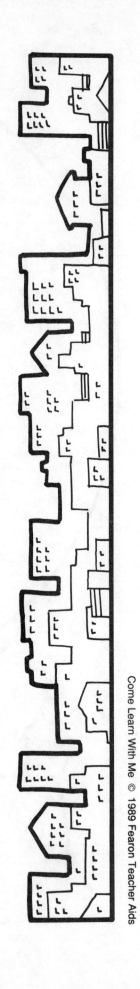

33

34

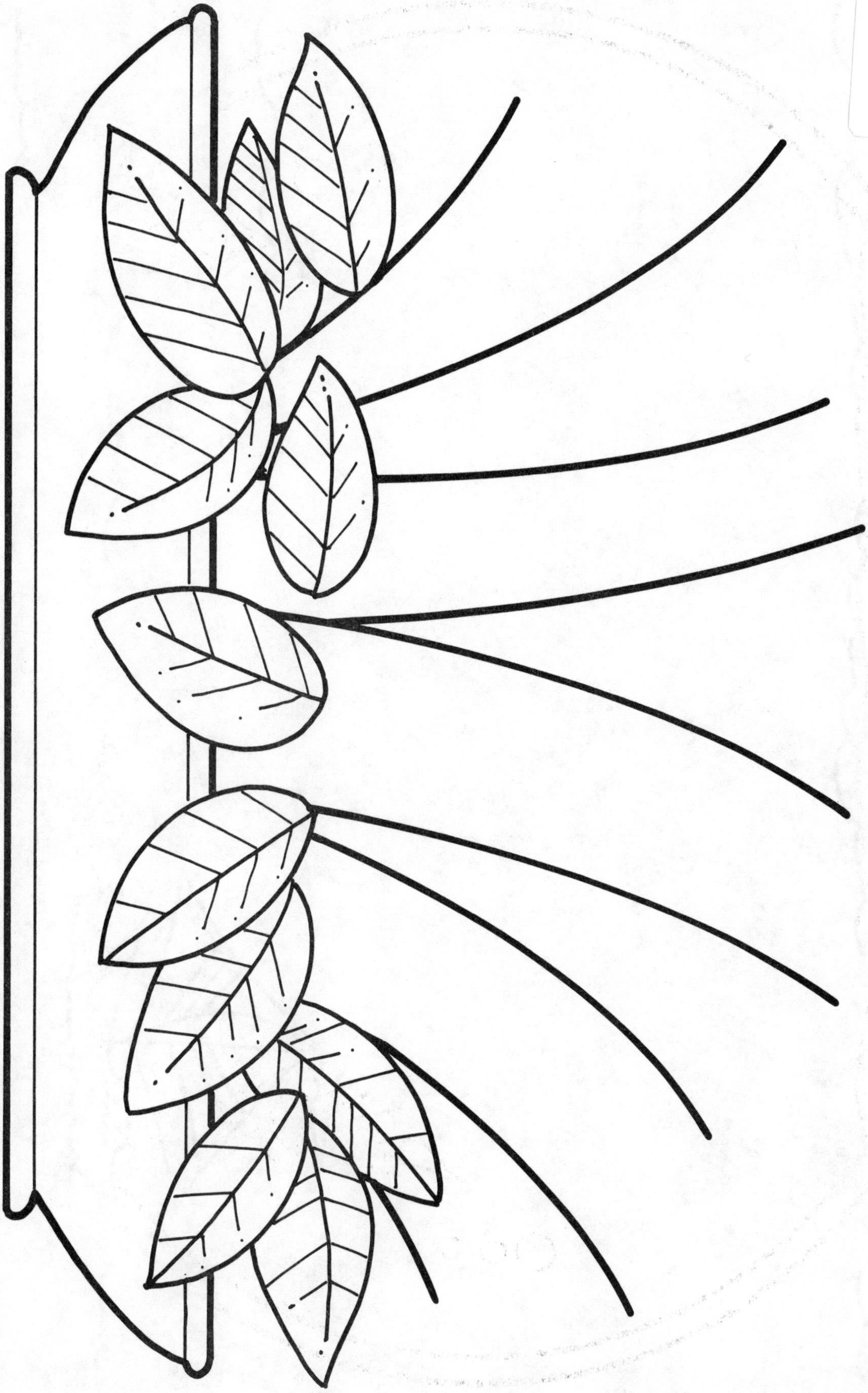

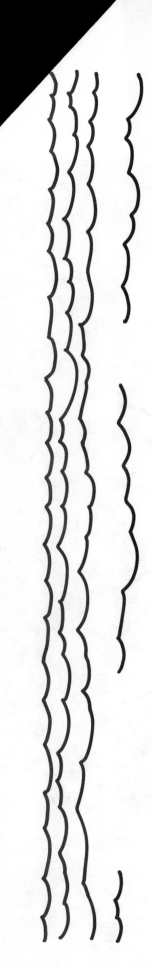

Daily Opening Activities

Flag Salute

Materials:

- a small flag for each child
- patriotic music

When all children have arrived, have each one get a flag. Instruct them to march in a circle and wave the flags to the patriotic music. Use this time to express some of the concepts you want to convey to children about the flag and America. "We show respect for our country and the flag by standing up when we see our flag. We stand up tall and straight when we hold our flag. We try not to let our flag touch the ground. These things show that we love America and that we are happy to live in this beautiful land." Have children hand you the flags to put away when the song has ended.

Prepare to say the "Pledge of Allegiance" with the children. Help children find their right hands to put over their hearts. It is helpful to put your left hand over your heart if you are facing the children, so they can copy your actions without confusion. Say the "Pledge of Allegiance" together. Say it slowly and distinctly so that the children can try to follow your mouth. Repetition and time will enable them to learn the words.

I pledge allegiance to the flag of the United States of America and to the republic for which it stands, one nation under God, indivisible with liberty and justice for all.

Who's Here?

Materials:

- name chart and figures

Display the name chart. Hold up children's figures one at a time, and let them try to recognize their own names. Have each child sit on your lap or stand beside you. Ask the child to put his or her figure in the pocket with the matching name. Help them as necessary. Sing the "Name Song" to each child after the figure has been placed on the chart. Give each child a big hug!

> **Name Song** (sing to tune of "The Farmer in the Dell")
> <u>(Child's name)</u> is here today.
> <u>(Child's name)</u> is here today.
> Let's all clap our hands and say, "<u>(Child's name)</u> is here today!"

Tell children individually that you love them and are glad they are at school today. Whatever comment you give, look into the child's eyes so it will be obvious you are giving your full attention to that child. If a child won't sit on your lap or come up beside you, sing the "Name Song" anyway and touch him or her gently as you speak. This is an important part of building a trusting relationship.

With larger groups you may want to have children come up three at a time. Or, have children put their names up as they arrive for school. This will give you the opportunity to speak with each child individually. Also, you can take each child's finger and point to the letters in his or her name and then point again to each letter of that child's name on the name chart.

Weather

Materials:

• weather chart
• children's clothes and weather symbols

Say to children, "Let's check the weather and get our weather children dressed." Take children outside or to the window. Talk about the color of the sky, the clouds, the warmth of the sun. Ask children if they can see the wind blowing. Then help them choose a weather symbol to put on the chart. Let students choose the appropriate clothes to dress the weather children. Point out how the clothes the children wore to school today are an indication of the weather outside.

With a larger group, use the "choosing chart" (suggested in the section describing how to make a fingerplay chart) to choose two students to dress the weather children.

Calendar

Materials:

• calendar and number emblems

Read the name of the month on the calendar, and have children repeat it. Say the days of the week while pointing to each one, and have children repeat them. Explain why a particular number emblem is being used: "In some places, January is a very cold time of year, so we are using snowflakes to decorate our calendar." Tell children which day of the week it is, and put up the appropriate number emblem. Have children repeat short sentences such as: "Today is _____." "Tomorrow is _____." "Yesterday was _____." Count slowly from the first day of the month to the current day. Point as you count. Say as much or as little about the calendar as there is interest.

Fingerplays

Materials:

• fingerplay chart

Have several children each take a figure from the chart. The fingerplays you put on the chart can either be from the lessons or other favorite fingerplays. After a while, children will develop favorites they want to do over and over. Children love repetition, and it is a good way for them to learn and gain confidence in their abilities.

Fall

■ Opening Activities
(pages 38–39)

■ Listen and Learn
- a green leaf
- autumn leaves
- "Animals Prepare for Winter" picture (page 43)
- flannel board

Ask children what they did during the summer, and tell some of your activities that relate to warm weather. "Our world is always changing. The season of fall is arriving." Discuss some of the unique characteristics of fall (weather gets cooler, leaves on the trees change color, etc.). Show the leaves you have collected. "The wind begins to blow, and the leaves start to **fall** off the trees. This is one way we can remember the name of this season." Do the following fingerplay with the children:

> Leaves are in the trees, red and green and brown.
> *(Wiggle your fingers.)*
> The wind is blowing treetops,
> *(Wave your arms back and forth.)*
> The leaves are falling down, down, down,
> *(Slowly let arms flutter down to the ground.)*
> 'Till they're resting on the ground.
> *(Rest arms and fingers on the ground.)*

Repeat several times.

Discuss with the children how the trees get ready for winter by dropping all the leaves off their branches. When the trees start dropping leaves and the weather starts getting cooler, the animals know it is time to get ready for winter. Put "Animals Prepare for Winter" picture on the flannel board. Many birds can't stand the cold weather. There are many places that get so cold it snows. Explain to children that this is the reason birds migrate to a warmer climate in preparation for the winter season. Also discuss how bears prepare for winter by eating more food, so they will be able to survive the winter when less food is available. Squirrels also prepare by storing a food supply. The remaining sections of this lesson focus on the bear, squirrel, and birds and their fall preparations for winter.

■ Storytime

Materials:

• "Teddy Bear's Winter Coat" or any short story about how animals
prepare for winter.

Ask children if their mothers or fathers have ever asked them to do something, and they were having so much fun playing or watching TV that they didn't want to do it. "This story is about a little bear who was too busy playing to do what he was told. Let's find out what happens to our little bear friend." Read the story.

■ Activities

NUT HUNT (GAME)

Materials:

• nuts (real or cut from construction paper)

Explain that squirrels prepare for winter by gathering a supply of nuts. Spread the nuts all around the floor of the room. Set a chair in the center of the room to represent the squirrels' home. "Let's pretend we are squirrels. We can see the leaves falling off the trees. We know it is time for us to gather lots of nuts. Let's see how quickly you little squirrels can gather the nuts and put them in our house for winter." Then say, "Go!" and have children pick up nuts and place them on the chair in the center of the room.

FLYING SOUTH (DRAMATIC PLAY)

Have children pretend to be birds sitting in a tree. Pretend that the leaves in the tree are changing from green to fall colors. Dramatize how the birds might feel and respond as the weather gets colder. "Let's get bunched up together to keep warm. It's getting much too cold for us here. Let's all fly away and find a warmer place to stay until winter is over." Continue to dramatize the trip as children "fly" to a warmer spot, saying, "Let's fly over this big mountain. Let's fly down and get a drink. Mmm! This water tastes good."

BEAR CAVE (DRAMATIC PLAY)
Materials:
• blanket (draped over a table for a bear cave)
Have children pretend to be bears. Talk about the signs of fall and how bears must eat lots of food in preparation for winter. Let children enjoy going in and out of the "bear cave."

FALL LEAVES (CRAFT)
Materials:
• "Fall Tree" activity page for each child (page 44)
• small sponge pieces
• fall colors of paint in shallow trays
Demonstrate how children can dip sponges in the paint and dab them on the tree branches to make colorful fall leaves. The fun is painting, so if children cover the entire paper, it's OK.

LEAF HUNT (OUTSIDE ACTIVITY)
Materials:
• lunch bag for each child
Have each child take a bag along on a "leaf hunt." Take a walk around the school grounds, and collect samples of the beautiful fall leaves that have fallen to the ground.

■ Closing
See if children can remember what happens to trees in the fall. This is not a test. If children can't remember, provide the answer. Then have children repeat the information back. Ask what the birds, squirrels, and bears do in the fall. Give hints if children can't remember (flap your arms or hold up a nut).

Animals Prepare for Winter

Fall

Fall Tree

I Was Born

■ Opening Activities

(pages 38–39)

■ Listen and Learn

Materials:

• a baby picture of you
• several pictures of children at various stages of growth

Begin by holding up the baby picture of yourself, and let children guess who it is! Remind children how special babies are and that everyone began life as a baby. Indicate with your hands the approximate size of a newborn baby. Ask children to lay on the floor and curl up very small, like a baby. Discuss the fact that babies are unable to do many things that these children are now capable of doing. Babies cannot talk. Ask children to think of ways babies communicate without words. Babies cannot move from place to place alone. Ask children how babies move. Ask children if babies can eat pizza or french fries, and see if they realize that babies are not born with teeth. Help children realize that newborn babies need a lot of care and love because they are incapable of doing things independently. Show pictures of children at various stages of growth. Talk about body size and other ways children change as they get older.

■ Storytime

Materials:

• "My First Day" or any short book about a newborn baby

Linda is a newborn baby who tells about her first experiences with her mother and father. "Pay special attention to how Linda's mother and father treat her as you listen to the story." Remember to either read the story or tell what is happening in each picture according to the attention span of the children. After the story ask children if they think their mothers and fathers treated them the same way when they were babies.

■ Activities

ROCK-A-BYE BABY (DRAMATIC PLAY)

Materials:

• a baby doll for each child (optional)

If baby dolls are not available, just have children pretend: "Let's pretend that we are the mommies and daddies. We just got our new babies. We need to hold them very gently in our arms. Oh, I can see that you make good mommies and daddies. Let's pretend we are taking the blanket off our babies so that we can count the fingers and toes. We will lay our babies very gently on the floor." Ask children if their babies are boys or girls. Pretend to count the fingers and toes. Continue dramatic play by feeding, burping, and rocking the babies. Sing "Rock-A-Bye Baby" or any other lullaby or favorite song as you rock the babies to sleep. Encourage participation by asking children why their babies are crying or what their babies' names are. Have children check their babies' diapers. Sometimes very young children won't do anything but watch. But as long as they are watching you take care of your pretend baby, they are learning. Enjoy yourself and the children will follow.

SLEEPING BABY (CRAFT)
Materials:
 For each child:
 • "Sleeping Baby" activity page (page 48)
 • small scrap of material for blanket
 • glue
 • crayons (optional)
 • wet sponge or rag for sticky fingers
Show children how to cover the sleeping baby with the blanket. Glue in place. Show the children how to dip a finger in the glue just once and not swirl it around. Gluing is a small motor skill and takes practice. Don't be surprised if you find yourself explaining how to use the glue correctly many times. You may have to hold a child's finger and practice dipping glue. Have the child also glue the bottle in place.

ALL ABOUT ME (CRAFT)
Materials:
 • "All About Me" activity page for each child (page 49)
 • magazine pictures of babies
 • glue
 • crayons
Lay out all of the baby pictures. Let children choose the ones they think look most like them as babies. Have them glue the pictures in the middle of their papers. After they have glued their baby pictures, show them the little girl and boy picture at the bottom of the page. Give each of the children a crayon and ask if they are boys or girls. They may not know. Show them which one to color. You may need to ask parents for the

information at the top of the page or let them fill it in when the papers are sent home. This lesson and the next four are all on a similar theme. These activity pages can be saved and made into individual student booklets when the unit is completed.

REMEMBER WHEN? (DRAMATIC PLAY)
Materials:
- bananas or baby food
- baby bottle or baby clothes

Let children crawl around and pretend to be babies themselves. Let them look at the baby clothes, try on a baby bootie, and eat baby food.

■Closing
"You were a very special baby to your mother and father when you were born, and now that you have grown from a little baby to a big girl or boy, you are still very special to your family."

Sleeping Baby

Cut along dotted line.

Cut bottle out for children to glue on their papers.

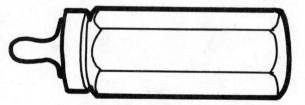

Come Learn With Me © 1989 Fearon Teacher Aids

I Was Born

All About Me

My name is _____

My birthday is _____

I am a little

boy   girl

(circle one)

I Was Born

I Am Growing

■ Opening Activities
(pages 38–39)

■ Listen and Learn
Materials:
- "Baby Hand and Footprints" picture (page 53)
- baby bootie or shoe (optional)

Review the discussion about babies from the last lesson.
Do the following action rhyme with the children:

> "Once I was so very small, now I'm growing tall, tall, tall."
> *(Have children stoop down as the poem begins and then grow
> to full size by the last "tall.")*
> Repeat several times.

There is much more to growing than just getting taller. Show children the
baby handprints and footprints. Allow them to compare the size of their
own hands and feet with the baby prints. Are they the same size? It may
be fun for children to try on a baby bootie. We are able to do so many
more things as we grow older. Ask children to name some things they are
able to do that little babies cannot do. And, of course, little babies don't
get to come to school!

■ Storytime
Materials:
- "The Shoes" or any short book about growing and changing

This story is about a little girl who loved her pretty shoes so much that
she continued to wear them when her feet grew too big to fit in them
anymore. "Listen to the story to see what problems the little girl has when
she wears shoes that are too small." Read the story.

■ Activities

How Big Am I? (COLORING)
Materials:
- "How Big Am I?" activity page for each child (page 54)
- bathroom scale
- yardstick or ruler
- crayons

50

Show children the scale and the yardstick, and explain how they are used to measure height and weight. Press your hand down on the scale so that children can see the numbers move in the window. Have children color their papers, while you measure each child's height and weight and record the information on the activity sheets. Be sure to save these papers for their booklets.

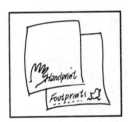

FOOT AND HANDPRINTS (CRAFT)
Materials:
- "My Footprint" and "My Handprint" pages for each child (pages 55–56)
- paint in a shallow tray (or crayons)
- water, soap, sponge, and towels for cleanup if paint is used

If you have a small group of children and a lot of patience, have children dip their hands and feet in a shallow tray of paint and make prints on their papers. For cleanup have a large piece of paper on the floor for children to blot off as much of the excess paint from their hands and feet as possible. Then let them wipe off the rest with a wet sponge or paper towels, or have a small amount of water for them to step in. One print for each page is enough. If you find this a bit too messy, have children use crayons to trace around their hands and feet on their papers.

BIRTHDAY PARTY! (GAMES)
Materials:
- "Clown Face" picture (page 57)
- one 1 1/2" red circle for each child
- tape
- beanbag
- balloons or other birthday items (optional)

"One of the fun things about getting bigger is that you have a birthday party." Pretend to have a birthday party and play some party games. Play any or all of the following party games.

Pin the Nose on the Clown
Blindfold children and let them try to get their red circles on the clown's face. Be sure to write the children's names on their circles before beginning the game.

Toss the Beanbag
Children sit on the floor and take turns catching the beanbag and throwing it back to you.

Duck, Duck, Goose

Children sit in a circle. One child is "It." "It" walks around the circle and taps each child on the head, saying "duck" each time. At any time, "It" may tap a child's head and say "goose." This child stands and chases "It" around the circle. "It" tries to make it all the way back around to the other child's place to sit down before being tagged.

Ring Around the Rosie

"Ring around the Rosie,
A pocketful of posies.
Ashes, ashes,
We all fall down!"

Children walk in a circle holding hands and singing. Then they "all fall down!"

London Bridge Is Falling Down

"London bridge is falling down, falling down, falling down.
London bridge is falling down, my fair lady."

Two children face each other, hold hands, and raise them overhead to form a bridge. The other children follow in a line, singing and going under the bridge. On "my fair lady," the two children who are the bridge lower their arms over the child who is under the bridge. Try variations of these games using balloons and other birthday items.

BIRTHDAY CAKE (CRAFT)

Materials:

- "My Birthday Cake" activity page for each child (page 58)
- enough birthday candles to represent each child's age (page 53)
- crayons
- glue
- wet sponge or rag for sticky fingers

Explain to children that one candle is put on a birthday cake for each year. Let children color their cakes, and help them glue on the correct number of candles. Save this page to be added to the special booklets.

■ Closing

"Growing up can be a lot of fun. There are so many new things for us to learn. We will be learning new things every day, and you will be growing older, taller, and smarter every day. That's exciting!"

Baby Hand and Footprints

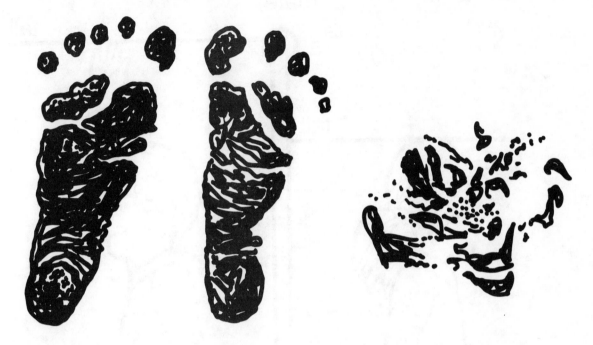

Explain: It is hard to get a handprint from a baby . . .

Cut on dotted line.

"My Birthday Cake" candle patterns

Cut candles and flames out of construction paper.

I Am Growing

How Big Am I?

As of _____ I am . . .

tall

tall

And I weigh _____

Name _____

I Am Growing

I'll keep these little handprints,
For some day you will see
These prints will be big handprints
And they'll still belong to me!

MY Handprints

I Am Growing

MY FOOTPRINTS

Come Learn With Me © 1989 Fearon Teacher Aids

I Am Growing

Clown Face

I Am Growing

My Birthday Cake

Happy Birthday

I am _____ years old.

I Belong to a Family

■ Opening Activities
(pages 38–39)

■ Listen and Learn
Materials:
- your family picture
- "Family Figures" (page 62)
- flannel board

Everyone belongs to a family. Talk a little bit about your family as you hold up the picture. Name family members and point to them. Put up the family figures on the flannel board and discuss each one. Discuss how some families are larger than others and consist of different people. Some families may have a single parent. Other families may have grandmothers and grandfathers living with them. Everyone in a family is special. Let each child come to the flannel board and put up the number of people in his or her family and name them. If it is a big group, the children will probably not be able to sit still long enough for everyone to have a turn. Allow time during the closing for others to name their family members. Do the following fingerplay with the children:

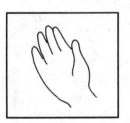

My Family
Here is daddy big and tall.
(Point to tallest, middle finger.)
Here is baby kind and small.
(Point to baby finger.)
Here is sister with her doll.
(Point to ring finger.)
Here is brother with his ball.
(Point to first finger.)
And here is mother who loves us all.
(Point to thumb and then wrap thumb around other fingers to make a fist.)

■ Storytime
Materials:
- "I Belong to a Family" or any other short story about families working together and caring for each other

This story is about a little girl named Danielle. She realizes that she is an important part of her family. "Listen to the story to see how Danielle's family helps her." Be sure to point out details as children enjoy the pictures. Read the story.

■ Activities

THE PEOPLE IN MY FAMILY (CRAFT)
Materials:
For each child:
- "The People in My Family" activity page (page 63)
- "Family Figures" (page 62)
- glue
- wet sponge or rag for sticky fingers

This page is about all the special people that make up a family. Have children think again of the people in their families. It would help if you knew ahead of time how many are in each child's family, so that you can give the proper number of family figures to glue on the houses. If you don't know, just ask children to name family members as best they can. Have children glue figures in place. Be sure to save these pages for the booklets to be compiled at the end of the unit.

FAMILY FUN (FINGER PUPPETS)
Materials:
- one set of "Family Finger Puppets" (page 64)

Discuss jobs that various family members have. Mothers may do laundry, cook dinner, go to work at an office, do the dishes, etc. Fathers may do yardwork, work at a business office, do the dishes, etc. Brothers and sisters may clean their rooms, take out the trash, take care of the baby, etc.

Have children use these ideas to answer the questions in the finger-play. Put the finger puppets on your fingers one at a time as you say the fingerplay.

The Finger Family's Good Morning
Good morning, Mother finger, what will you do today?
I'll ____, that's what I'll do today.
Good morning, Father finger, what will you do today?
I'll ____, that's what I'll do today.
Good morning, Brother finger, what will you do today?
I'll ____, that's what I'll do today.
Good morning, Sister finger, what will you do today?
I'll ____, that's what I'll do today.
Good morning, Baby finger, what will you do today?
I'll ____, that's what I'll do today.

If children cannot think of jobs to fill in the blanks, fill them in yourself, and they will catch on to the idea.

Big or Little (sorting)
Materials:
- "Big and Little Family Figures" (page 65)

Cut apart the family figures and mix them all up. Have children help you sort all of the big people in one pile and the little people in another pile. Demonstrate and help as necessary. Use the words "big" and "little" as often as possible, and encourage children to tell you if a figure is big or little. Remember, concepts that seem easy to you need to be developed and learned. Repetition is fun for children and serves to increase their confidence in themselves.

■ Closing
"We need big people like mommies, daddies, aunts, uncles, and grandparents in our families. We also need little people like you. You are a special member of your family!!"

Family Figures

I Belong to a Family

The People in My Family

I Belong to a Family

Family Finger Puppets

Cut in slightly so that head will not wrap around finger.

I Belong to a Family

Big and Little
Family Figures

I Belong to a Family

Names

■ Opening Activities
(pages 38–39)

■ Listen and Learn

Materials:

• picture of each child's family (optional)

Ask each child to tell you his or her name. Help any child who has difficulty by saying it and having the child repeat after you. Compliment children for any attempts to speak. See if children can also tell you the names of their brothers and sisters if they have any. If possible, have a picture of each child's family so that the child can point out and name each member. Explain that some people are called by more than one name. Using yourself as an example, say, "The children at school call me Teacher. I have another name. My name is _____." Some people have nicknames also. Names are important. They help us know whom we are talking about.

■ Storytime

Materials:

• "Paul Gets Lost" or any other short story about the importance of names

This story is about a little boy named Paul who gets lost in a store. He realizes that to find his mother, it is important to know her name. "Listen to the story, and try to remember how Paul finally finds his mother." Read or tell the story. After the story look again at the pictures, and compare the different mothers. Have children tell the story back to you by looking at each picture.

■ Activities

LOOK AT ME! (CRAFT)

Materials:

• "Me" activity page for each child (page 68)
• crayons
• mirror (optional)

Draw a picture of each of the children. They can look at themselves in the mirror while you draw. Have each child stand by you and tell you about how he or she looks. If a child cannot tell you, you can say, "You have two eyes, a big smile, long blonde hair, etc." Talk while you draw.

At the bottom of the page, write the child's name and explain that this is how the name looks. Use a capital letter only at the beginning of the name. This is how they will be taught in kindergarten. Let children color their pictures and tape them up on the wall.

NAME MATCH (GAME)

Materials:
- one 2" x 8" paper strip for each child with their name printed on it
- tape

Show children the name strips. Be sure each child knows what his or her name looks like. Hold each child's finger to point to the letters as you spell the child's name. Point to the pictures from the previous activity that are taped on the wall. Have children match their name strips to the pictures on the wall. Help children as necessary. Praise them for their accomplishments. If you have a large group, let two or more children try at the same time, and have the other children clap and give encouragement.

"ALL ABOUT ME" BOOK COVER (CRAFT)

Materials:
For each child:
- 12" x 18" construction paper
- little boy or girl figure (page 80)
- crayons
- glue
- children's photos of themselves from home (optional)

Give each child a boy or girl figure to color and glue on the front of the folded construction paper. Pictures from home can be glued on also. This will be the cover for the special booklets created in the past few lessons. Write their names on the covers. Or write them on pieces of paper for children to glue on the covers. When this unit is completed, put all the activity papers in the covers.

■ Closing

Do a favorite fingerplay or sing a song. "You did so well today. We will keep practicing finding your names. Soon it will be easy to find your name every time!"

Me

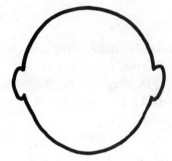

Come Learn With Me © 1989 Fearon Teacher Aids

Names

My Wonderful Body _____

■ Opening Activities
(pages 38–39)

■ Listen and Learn
Discuss with the children how our bodies have many parts. Call out the names of larger parts of the body, and have children move them (arms, legs, head). Call out the names of smaller parts of the body, and have children move them (fingers, toes, eyes, lips). Also point out that everyone has two eyes, two ears, two hands, and two feet. Do the following fingerplay with the children:
(Point to the body part that is mentioned in each line.)

My Body Can Do Wonderful Things
My little eyes can see pretty things.
My little nose smells something good.
My little ears hear someone sing.
My little mouth tastes yummy food.

You may want to do this several times, and after the first line mention some of the pretty things you like to see. Ask children what pretty things their eyes can see. Do the same with each line.

■ Storytime
Materials:
• "I Want a Body" or any short story about how wonderfully our bodies are made and all that they allow us to do.
This story is about a little ghost named Mickey whose wish to have a body is granted by the Wishing Star. Mickey obtains one part of his new body at a time. "Listen carefully to the story, and try to guess which part of his body Mickey gets first and second and third." Read the story.

■ Activities

MY FACE (CRAFT)
Materials:
• "My Face" activity page for each child (page 71)
• crayons
• lipstick
• tissues

We all have the same body parts, and yet each of us is unique. Point out how everyone has two eyes, but not everyone has the same color of eyes. Point out how hair color and style vary. Discuss how smiles and laughter are unique. Give children crayons for the color of their eyes. Have children color the eyes on the papers. Then give them the color of crayon for their hair. Show children where to color the hair on their pictures. Put lipstick on children's lips, and have them kiss their papers to make lip prints. Demonstrate how they are to do this. Give them a tissue to wipe off their lips when finished. Do each item one at a time. It is difficult for children to remember more than one instruction at a time. Be sure to save the page for their booklets!

CLAY (CRAFT)

Materials:

• one small ball of clay for each child

Let each child play with a ball of clay. With your clay, roll a ball for a head and a ball for a body. Roll out arms and legs. As you play with the children, tell them that you are going to make a body out of clay. "I have a round ball for the head. Here is an oval shape for the body. I'm going to put the head on the body. Now where do you think these arms should go? Where should I put the legs? Would you like to make a body with your clay?" Roll out parts for the children. Encourage them to put a clay body together by themselves, regardless of how it turns out. Working with clay is very good for small muscle coordination.

Use the tune to "Here We Go Round the Mulberry Bush" for this action verse:

> **This Is the Way!**
> This is the way we wash the dishes,
> Wash the dishes, wash the dishes,
> This is the way we wash the dishes,
> So early in the morning.

Try using other verses such as: "This is the way we play with our clay . . ." or "This is the way we hop on one foot . . ." Allow children to think of new verses.

■ Closing

Assemble each child's booklet of pages that have been collected over the past few days. Allow children to take their booklets home to share with friends and family.

My Face

The color of my hair is _____

The color of my eyes are _____

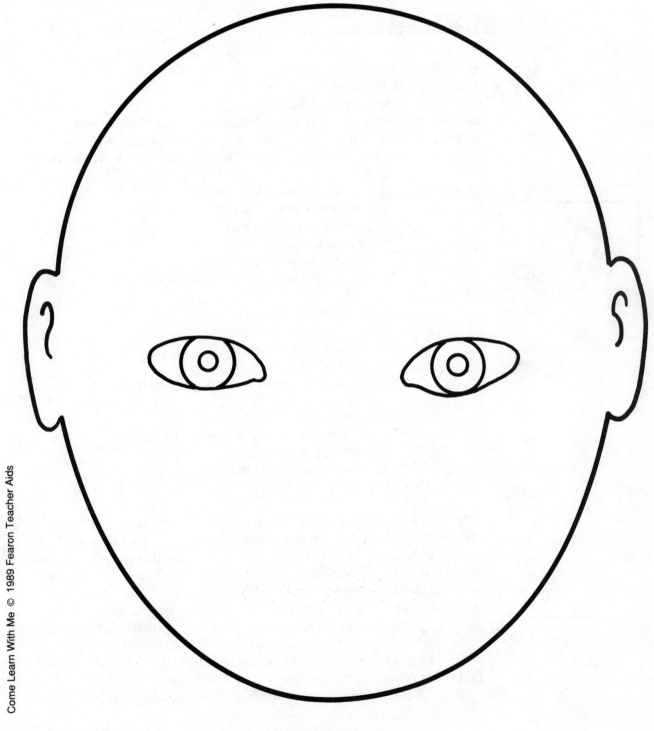

My Wonderful Body

Come Learn With Me © 1989 Fearon Teacher Aids

The Sense of Sight

■ Opening Activities
(pages 38–39)

■ Listen and Learn

Materials:
• blindfold
• "I Want a Body" story
• flower and star pictures (page 75)

Remind children of the story about Mickey in the last lesson. Read the story again, look at the pictures, or have children tell the parts they remember. Sing the following song to the tune of "Polly Wolly Doodle":

(Point to the body parts as they are mentioned.)

It's My Body and I Love It

Oh, I have two eyes I can see a lot,
Seeing pretty, pretty sights all day.
My nose it is the greatest nose,
Smelling yummy, yummy smells all day.

Chorus:

Hip-hoo-ray, Hip-hoo-ray!
Hip-hoo-ray, for me today!
It's my body and I love it.
It's my body and I love it.
Feelin' happy, happy feelings all the day.

Oh, I have two ears I can hear a lot,
Hearing happy, happy sounds all the day.
My mouth it is the greatest mouth,
Tasting goody, goody things all the day.

(Repeat chorus)

"Our eyes help us to do things every day. Let's see what our eyes can help us do." Ask one of the children to come up and take off a shoe. If no one will, take off your own shoe. "Let's pretend that we just woke up, and it is time to get dressed for breakfast." Put the shoe a short distance from the child helping you, and say, "You have all of your clothes on except for one shoe. Can you use your eyes to help you find your shoe?" Have the child pick up the shoe. To show how important our eyes are, repeat the activity, but this time cover the child's eyes with a blindfold. Put the shoe a short distance away, and ask the child to feel around to find it. Let other children try this activity if they want.

Have children name some of the beautiful things they can see with their eyes in the daytime. Then hold up the picture of the flowers. Ask children to name some things they see at night. Hold up the star picture. Have children close their eyes. Then hold up either the star or flower picture again. Ask children to tell you which picture is in view without using their eyes. Let them guess and then open their eyes to see if they guessed right. Continue according to the interest of the children. "Aren't eyes a wonderful part of our bodies?"

■ Storytime

Materials:
- "What Can You See?" flannel board story and figures or a story of your choice that emphasizes how useful our eyes are
- flannel board
- tape to attach figures to flannel board

This story is about a little boy named Clinton who goes to visit his grandparents. Clinton and his grandpa go on a walk and notice how many things they can see with their eyes. "Listen carefully to find out if you have ever seen the things that Clinton sees on his walk." Have children hold the flannel board figures, and put them up at the appropriate times during the story.

■ Activities

BLIND CATCH (GAME)
Materials:
- beanbag

"Eyes are useful when we are playing. Let's play catch with a beanbag." Have children sit in a circle, throw the beanbag to them, and have them throw it back. Let each child have a turn. Now have children close their eyes and try to catch the beanbag. Give each child a turn. You will probably have to keep reminding children to close their eyes. Warn them before you throw the beanbag. Discuss whether it was easier to catch the beanbag with their eyes opened or closed.

LOOK WHAT I SEE! (DRAMATIC PLAY)
"Let's take a walk like Clinton and his grandpa. We can take turns telling each other what we can see with our wonderful eyes!" Walk around the room or outside. Encourage children to wait their turn so that everybody can hear and have a chance to tell what they see.

EYE PUPPET (CRAFT)

Materials:

- "Eye Puppet" pieces for each child (page 76)
- crayons
- glue
- wet sponge or rag for sticky fingers

Fold paper strip on the dotted line. Demonstrate for children how to glue the opened eyes underneath the folded flap and the closed eyes on the top of the flap. Have them draw a mouth below the eyes and color the puppets. Now the children can open and close their puppet's eyes by moving the flap.

■ Closing

"Eyes are a wonderful part of our body. It was fun talking about them. Use your eyes today to notice all the pretty things around you."

Stars

Flowers

The Sense of Sight

Eye Puppet Pattern

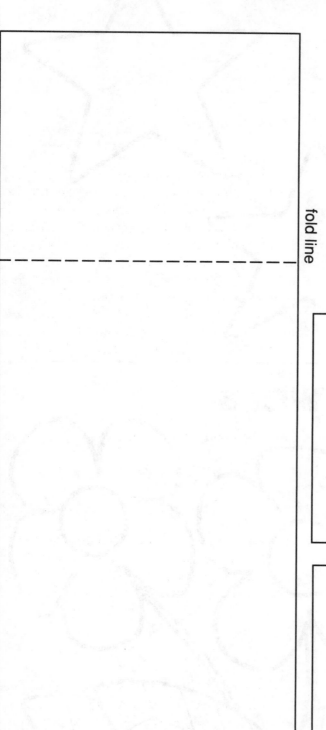

fold line

Baby is sleeping . . . oh, so sound.

Open your eyes and look around.

The Sense of Sight

The Sense of Hearing

■ Opening Activities
(pages 38–39)

■ Listen and Learn
Materials:
• an assembled "Cuckoo Clock" (page 81)
Have children point to their ears. Discuss the wonderful things our ears allow us to hear. The following activity will help children realize that we can identify something by the sound it makes. Have children close their eyes, put their hands over them, and put their heads down on their laps. Ask children to identify your actions using only the sense of hearing. Clap your hands. Then sing and stomp your feet. Try doing three actions in a row such as whistling, sniffing, and then clapping. Other suggestions for sounds are snapping your fingers, humming, or making animal noises.

Bring out the cuckoo clock and say, "This is a special clock because it has a little cuckoo bird inside that says 'cuckoo' every hour. Listen to the rhyme about my cuckoo clock." Swing the pendulum back and forth as you say the rhyme:

Tic Tock
Tic tock, tic tock, I'm a little cuckoo clock.
Tic tock, tic tock, Uh oh! It's one o'clock. "Cuckoo."
Tic tock, tic tock, I'm a little cuckoo clock.
Tic tock, tic tock, Uh oh! It's two o'clock.
"Cuckoo, cuckoo."
Repeat with three o'clock, etc.

As you say "cuckoo," lift up the cuckoo window. Children can sit on their knees or cross-legged and rock back and forth in rhythm as they say the rhyme. Have them stop rocking as they say, "Uh oh! It's one o'clock." Then have children lean over so that they can pop up and say, "Cuckoo!"

■ Storytime
Materials:
• "Where is my Kitty?" or any short story about ears or identifying sounds
This story is about a little boy named Sam who searches for his lost kitty. He listens to sounds and tries to identify his Kitty's cry. "Try to help Sam guess what makes the sounds he hears." Read the story.

■ Activities

WHO IS SPEAKING? (GAME)
Materials:
- assembled "Sally and Freddie" puppets (page 80)

Use a high voice to introduce Sally to the children. Use a low voice to introduce Freddie. Then have children close their eyes, cover them with their hands, and put their heads down on their laps. Alternate having the two puppets say different things in high or low voices. Let children guess who is speaking.

POPSICLE STICK PUPPETS (CRAFT)
Materials:
For each child:
- "Sally and Freddie" puppets (page 80)
- two popsicle sticks
- glue
- crayons

Cut out and glue the puppets on the popsicle sticks before they are given to the children. Have children color Sally and Freddie.

PUPPET TALK (DRAMATIC PLAY)
Materials:
- Sally and Freddie puppets the children made previously

Demonstrate again how Sally speaks in a high voice and Freddie speaks in a low voice. Ask children to use high and low voices with their puppets.

CUCKOO CLOCK (CRAFT)
Materials:
For each child:
- "Cuckoo Clock" pattern (page 81)
- brad fastener
- glue
- wet sponge or rag for sticky fingers
- crayons

Have children match the face of the clock with the circle on the clock and glue it in place. Remember to avoid correcting children's projects if they don't glue things in exactly the right place. Help them glue on the flap of the door and place it over the cuckoo bird. (If the whole door is glued down, it will not open!) Then help them put the pendulums on with the fastener, or you can put them on in advance. Do the "Tic Tock" action rhyme again. Show children how to rock the pendulum and lift up the little door for the cuckoo bird.

■Closing

"We have very special bodies. Our ears help us to hear all of the sounds around us. When you go home today, see how many different sounds you can hear around your house."

Sally and Freddie

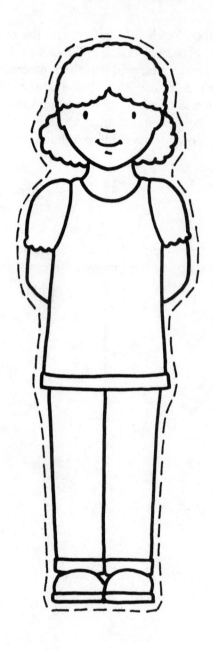

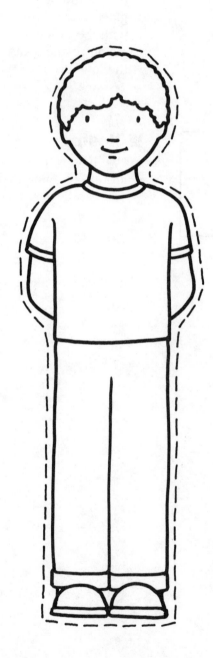

Color, cut out, and glue on popsicle sticks to make two puppets.

The Sense of Hearing

Come Learn With Me © 1989 Fearon Teacher Aids

Cuckoo Clock

The Sense of Hearing

The Sense of Touch

■ Opening Activities
(pages 38–39)

■ Listen and Learn
Materials:
• trace and cut out your handprints
Place the hands on the flannel board as an introduction to the topic. Explain to children that you will be talking about some of the wonderful things our hands do. Begin with the following fingerplay:

My Hands
My hands can say hello.
(Wave hello with one hand.)
My hands can say goodbye.
(Wave goodbye with the other hand.)
My hands can say, "I love you."
(Cross your chest with your hands.)
You are *(Point to children.)* my friend *(Point to yourself.)*
That's why!
Repeat several times.

■ Storytime
Materials:
• "Under the Bed" or any short story about hands or identifying something by touch

This story is about a little boy named Tony who uses his sense of touch to find his lost shoe. "Listen carefully to the story, and see where Tony finally finds his shoe." Children can participate during the story by helping Tony guess what he is feeling. Read the story.

■ Activities

FEEL AND GUESS (GAME)
Materials:
• two small paper bags
• items such as small toys, spoons, cups, brushes, and crayons

Put all the items in one bag. Transfer one item into the empty bag behind your back so that children cannot see which item it is. Discuss how we do not always use just our eyes to tell what things are. We can use our hands to feel and discover. Have one child come up and reach in the bag. Ask the child to feel the item and guess what it is. If the child will not or cannot speak well enough to tell what the item is, give praise anyway: "You did such a good job at sticking your hand in the bag. Pull it out and show everybody what you found!" Change the item in the bag, and let other children have turns. It's OK to repeat items also. Children enjoy repetition, and it makes it easier to succeed.

TOUCH AND FEEL (CRAFT)
Materials:

For each child:
- "Touch and Feel" activity page (page 84)
- small piece of furry cloth
- small piece of sandpaper
- sticker
- feather
- glue
- wet sponge or rag for sticky fingers

Have a "Touch and Feel" book made up ahead of time according to the directions below. Read the book with the children and let them feel it and repeat the words after you. "Would you like to make your own book to feel?" Pass out materials, and let children glue items in the proper spots on the pages. Remember, these are their booklets, and your concern is more "process" than finished product. After they have glued on all of the items, cut their papers into fourths, and staple to make booklets.

GUESS WHAT I FEEL? (GAME)
Materials:
- blindfold

This is another activity using the hands to feel and identify. Demonstrate by putting the blindfold over your eyes. Touch something within your reach, and guess what it is. Try touching the children. "I think I feel some nice long hair." Let children take turns being blindfolded. If any child is uncomfortable with the blindfold, use your hand as a blindfold, and direct his or her hand to something or someone to feel and identify.

■ Closing
Materials:
- fingerplay chart

"Let's use our wonderful hands and fingers to do some fingerplays." Use the chart to select some fingerplays to do with the children.

Touch and Feel

Stickers feel "smooth."

Furry Teddy Bears are "soft."

Bird feathers are also "soft."

But Daddy's beard feels "rough."

The Sense of Touch

Come Learn With Me © 1989 Fearon Teacher Aids

The Sense of Taste

■ Opening Activities
(pages 38–39)

■ Listen and Learn
Materials:
• flannel board figures of apple, orange, and lemon (page 88)

"Do you all have a mouth? Do you all have a tongue? Can you open your mouth really wide and stick out your tongue?" Discuss with the children how we use our tongues for talking, singing, and best of all, for tasting delicious food! Our tongues tell us that potato chips are salty, lemons are sour (pantomime eating a lemon, and pucker your mouth in response), and candy is sweet. Allow children to tell about a time when their tongues "told them something." Use the flannel board figures and do the following action rhyme with the children (It has a singsong rhythm to it.):

Way up high in the apple tree,
(Point up in the air.)
Two little apples were looking at me.
(Make circles with fingers and look through them.)
I shook that tree as hard as I could,
(Pretend to shake the tree.)
Down came an apple,
(Point to treetop and bring hand down as if an apple were falling out of the tree.)
Mmm! Was it good!
(Pretend to take a bite out of the apple, and with a look of delight, rub your tummy.)

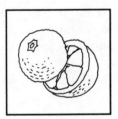

Way up high in the orange tree,
Two little oranges were looking at me.
I shook that tree as hard as I could,
Down came an orange,
Mmm! Was it good!

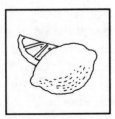

Way up high in the lemon tree,
Two little lemons were looking at me.
I shook that tree as hard as I could,
Down came a lemon,

(With a face of anticipation of the delicious taste, pretend to bite into the lemon, and then show a sour face.)
Oooo! Was it sour!

■ Storytime

Materials:

• "Ice Cream" or any short story about foods we enjoy tasting

This story is about a little boy named Johnnie who tries to guess what tasty surprise his mother is bringing him from the grocery store. "Listen carefully to the story to find out if Johnnie guesses right." Read the story.

■ Activities

ICE CREAM CONES (CRAFT)

Materials:

For each child:

• brown ice cream cone (page 88)
• two ice cream cone scoops (page 88)
• glue
• wet sponge or rag for sticky fingers

Have children glue the scoops on their cones. Talk about their favorite flavors.

FOODS I LIKE (CRAFT)

Materials:

• "Foods I Like" activity paper for each child (page 89)
• crayons

Hold a copy of the "Foods I Like" paper. Have children name the foods you point to. If children don't know, just tell them. Pass out the papers, and instruct children to color the foods that they like to eat. Coloring is a skill that is being developed, so don't be surprised if everything is just scribbled over.

ALL MIXED UP! (SORTING)

Materials:

• activity page with food and tools for each child (page 90)

This activity will take some preparation on your part. Cut out the tool box and grocery bag on the dotted line. Staple them at the bottom of the blank section to form two pockets. Label one side "Foods" and the other side "Tools." Cut apart the food and tool pictures, and keep them clipped together or in a baggie. Pass out a pocket chart and the pictures to each child. "The groceries were sitting on the counter. The tool box was on the floor next to the counter. Kitty rubbed against the groceries, knocked them over, and all of the food and tools got mixed together." Ask children to put the tools in the tool box and the food back in the grocery bag by sorting the pictures in the correct pockets.

Tasting Time (game)
Materials:
• samples of a food (raisins, peanuts, crackers, or grapes)
Have children close their eyes and try the food items. Ask children to guess what they are eating using only the sense of taste. When they guess right, be sure to tell the children what smart tongues they have!

■ Closing
"I had fun today talking about our tongues. They're another part of our wonderful bodies." Sing "It's My Body and I Love It" (page 72).

Flannel Board Figures

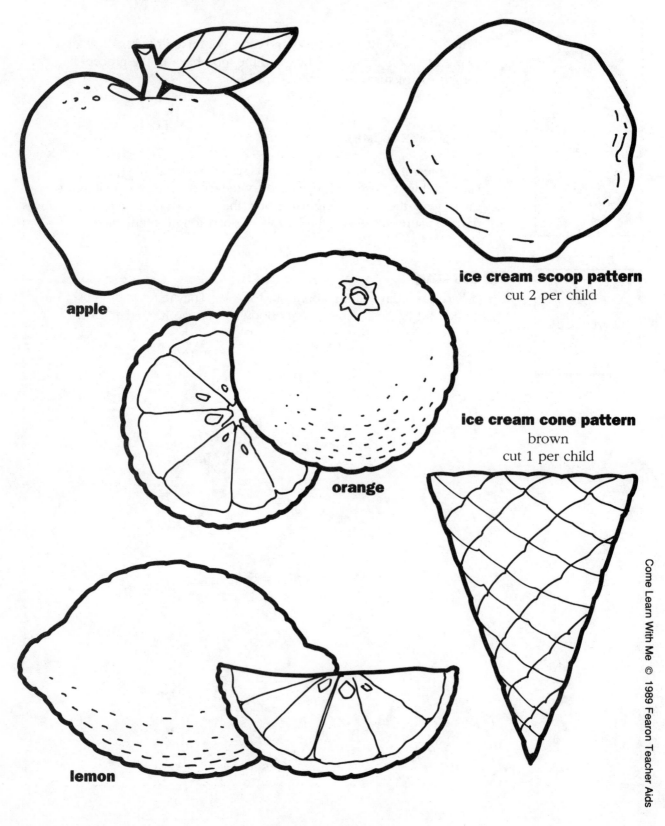

apple

ice cream scoop pattern
cut 2 per child

orange

ice cream cone pattern
brown
cut 1 per child

lemon

The Sense of Taste

Foods I Like

Color the foods you like to eat.

potato

carrot

apple

milk

ice cream

orange

grape

bread

banana

strawberry

The Sense of Taste

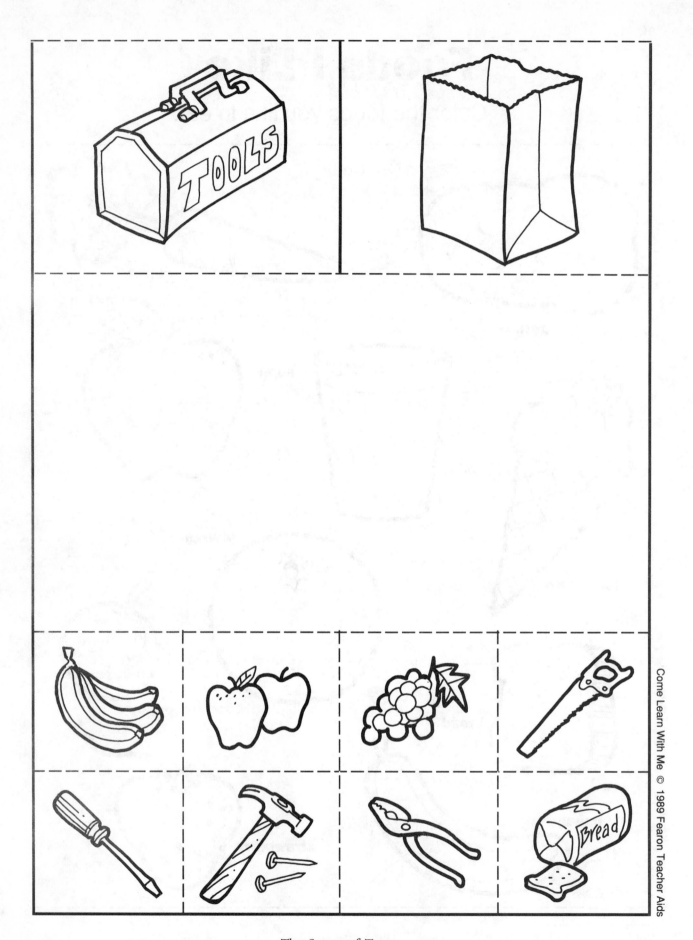

The Sense of Taste

Come Learn With Me © 1989 Fearon Teacher Aids

The Sense of Smell _____

■ Opening Activities

(pages 38–39)

■ Listen and Learn

Give children hints, and let them guess what part of the body this lesson is about. "This part of our body is right in the middle of our faces. We use it to smell things." Give children time to respond, or go back over the hints and make them very obvious. Do the following fingerplay with the children:

> I have a nose.
> It sits in the middle of my face.
> *(Touch nose with both hands.)*
> This is exactly the very best place for my nose.
> It can smell.
> *(Take a deep breath while sniffing.)*
> It works very, very, well!
> *(Tap your nose.)*

Repeat several times.

■ Storytime

Materials:

• "It Smells Good" or any short story about identifying smells

"Do you ever get really hungry, but your mother says you have to wait until dinnertime before you can eat? When I am really hungry, I can smell the food cooking, and it makes me even more hungry. Does that ever happen to you?" Give children a chance to share their experiences. The little girl in the story plays a smelling game. Tell children that if they listen closely, they can find out how to play the smelling game, too. Read the story.

■ Activities

SMELL AND MATCH (CRAFT)

Materials:

For each child:
• "Smell and Match" activity page (page 93)
• grape-, banana-, strawberry-, and flower-scented stickers
• crayons

Ask children to smell each sticker and then stick it on the matching picture. Have them color the pictures as well.

SMELLING WALK (OUTSIDE ACTIVITY)

Take children outside. Smell the grass, leaves, dirt, flowers, and air. Scents are often stronger if you crush the leaves, flower, or grass in your hand.

WHAT SMELLS GOOD? (CRAFT)

Materials:

- "What Smells Good?" activity page for each child (page 94)
- glue
- wet sponge or rag for sticky fingers
- crayons (optional)

Cut apart the pictures on the bottom of the page for each child. "This boy's name is Charlie. The pictures are some of Charlie's favorite things to smell." Have children match Charlie's favorites and glue them on the pages. Encourage discussion about their favorite things to smell. Children can color the pages when they are completed.

■ Closing

Sing "It's My Body and I Love It" (page 72) or do a favorite fingerplay. "When you go home tonight, play the smelling game and guess what you will be having for dinner."

Smell and Match

The Sense of Smell

What Smells Good?

The Sense of Smell

Good Manners

■ Opening Activities
(pages 38–39)

■ Listen and Learn

Materials:
• assembled pair of "Good-Manner Birds" (page 97)
This lesson centers around the words "please" and "thank-you." Ask children if they use these good-manner words, and encourage them to talk about specific examples. Explain that using good manners makes others happy. Discuss appropriate times to use these words. "I brought two friends with me today. They are my good-manner birds. I have a poem to tell you about them."

> Two good-manner birds sitting in trees.
> They always say thank-you, they always say please.
> *(Tip birds toward each other, as if they are talking.)*
> They will fly for you if you say please.

Children say the next two lines:

> Please fly away.
> *(With a swooshing sound make them fly away behind your back.)*
> Please come back.
> *(With a swooshing sound make the birds come back.)*
> Special magic words are these.

Repeat the poem several times.
"Good-manner words like 'please' and 'thank-you' are magic words because they make people feel like helping you when you use them."

■ Storytime

Materials:
• "Mother's Face" or any short story about using good manners
This story is about a little boy named Johnny who forgets to use good manners. "Listen carefully to the story and find out if Johnny finally remembers how to say please and thank-you." As you read, use the facial expressions that the mother makes in the book. Ask children if the face you are making is happy or sad. Point out details in the pictures.

■ Activities

GOOD MANNERS CATCH (GAME)
Materials:
• ball or beanbag
Have children sit in a circle in a straddle position. One at a time, have the children say to you, "Please roll me the ball." Roll the ball, or throw the beanbag. When a child catches, encourage a "thank-you." It is important for children to say more than just the word "please." They need to ask correctly for what they want. If all they can say is "Ball, please," that will do also. Prompt children as necessary. Praise them for being so polite. Give each child several turns. Be free with your praise. "You did it! It makes me feel so happy to hear you using good-manner words."

GOOD-MANNER BIRDS (CRAFT)
Materials:
For each child:
• "Good-Manner Bird" pieces (page 97)
• two popsicle sticks
• black crayon
• glue
• wet sponge or rag for sticky fingers
Each child will be making two good-manner birds. Trace and cut out the bird bodies and wings on blue construction paper. Trace and cut out the beaks on orange paper. Glue the bird bodies on the popsicle sticks for the children. Give each child two of everything. Show children how to glue on the wings and beak for each bird. If they glue any part in the wrong place, do not fix it. These are their projects. Use encouraging comments: "I like it. You did it all by yourself." After the pieces are all glued in place, children can draw on a black eye. Let children use the good-manner birds as you say the poem on page 95 again.

MORE PLEASE? (DRAMATIC PLAY)
Materials:
• snack item such as crackers
Have a pretend or real snack party to allow children a chance to practice their good-manner words. Be sure to compliment children when they say, "May I have some more crackers, **please?**"

■ Closing

"Thank-you for being so polite today! Take your good-manner birds home, and they will remind you to use words like 'please' and 'thank-you.'" Encourage children to use the good-manner words at home.

Good-Manner Bird Pattern

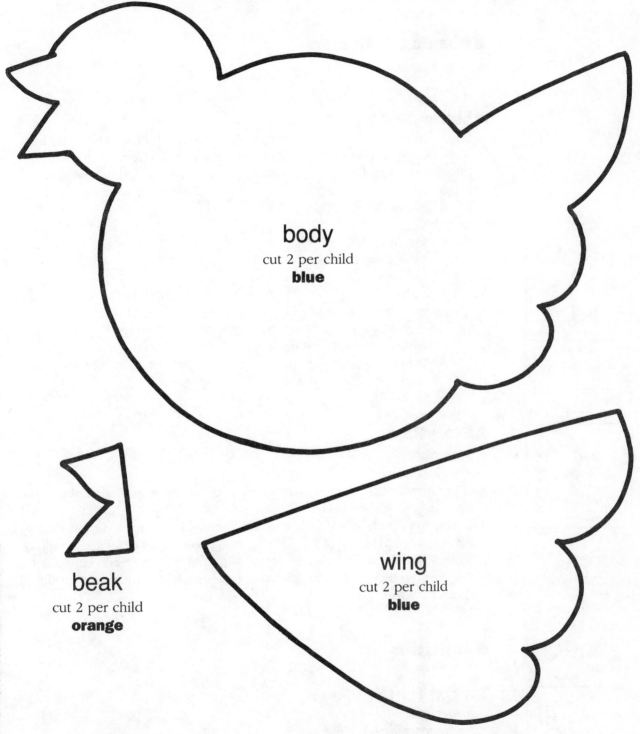

body
cut 2 per child
blue

beak
cut 2 per child
orange

wing
cut 2 per child
blue

Glue bird on a popsicle stick to make a puppet.

On and Off _____

■ Opening Activities

(pages 38–39)

■ Listen and Learn

"On" and "Off" are the two words being discussed today. Have children repeat these words after you. Praise them for their efforts. Begin with the following fingerplay: "Everyone hold up your hands and wiggle your fingers. When your hands are up and your fingers are wiggling, then I know you are ready to begin."

On and Off
I place my fingers **on** my nose.
On my head and knees and toes.
I place my fingers **on** my nose, now I take them **off** my nose and put them **on** my head.
Now I take them **off** my head, and put them on my knees.
Now I take them **off** my knees, and put them **on** my toes.
Let children say it with you the first time. Then try altering the pace by saying it really quickly or slowly.

■ Storytime

Materials:

• flannel board
"Get On, Get Off" flannel board story and figures or any other short story that deals with the two words "on" and "off."

This story is about a little boy named Jimmy. He seems to be **on** things that he shouldn't be, and he is always being told to get **off**. Pass out the flannel board figures for children to hold. Tell them to listen carefully to the story, so they will know when to come up and put the figure **on** the flannel board.

■ Activities

TOY ON, TOY OFF (GAME)
Materials:

• one toy for each child
Demonstrate how the game is played by being the first player. Call a child's name, and ask that child to put his or her toy "**on** the chair." Call another child, and say, "Put your toy **on** the floor." When all children have been given a direction, count to three, and everyone can run to take

their toys **off** and come sit back on the floor with them. Play the game again, and choose a child to give directions. Prompt children to use "please," "thank-you," and "on."

Crowns (Craft)
Materials:
For each child:
- "Crown" (page 100)
- two 1" x 8" paper strips
- tape
- crayons
- glue
- wet sponge or rag for sticky fingers
- small paper shapes (optional)

"We are going to make crowns to go **on** our heads." Let children color the crowns or glue on small paper shapes. Children love to rub their fingers around and around in the glue. Help them learn to just dip one finger in the glue for greater efficiency. Practice is the best way to gain the skill. Staple a paper strip on each side of the crown. Fit the crown around the child's head, and staple strips together. Make an elaborate production of actually putting on the finished crowns. "Everyone get ready. Let's count to three together. 1, 2, 3, **ON!** Aren't we beautiful!"

On the Couch (Game)
Materials:
- favorite book

Assemble all of the children together on a couch, rug area, or whatever you have available. Ask, "Is (child's name) **on** the couch?" Let the indicated child answer. When all have had a chance to answer, read them a favorite book.

Simon Says (Game)
This familiar game is good for practicing "on" and "off." Simon says, "Put your hands **on** your head." Simon says, "Take your hands **off** your head." Use other directions that ask children to put "on" or take "off."

■Closing
Remind children to practice the words learned today as well as the good-manner words. Ask children to notice if they hear other people using these words.

Crown

Staple strip here.

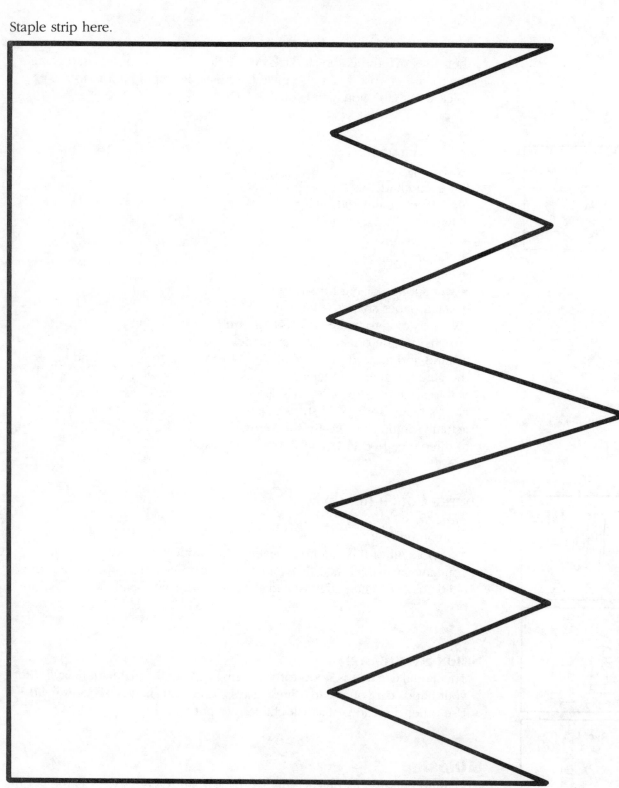

Staple strip here.

On and Off

Learning to Brush Our Teeth _____

■ Opening Activities

(pages 38–39)

■ Listen and Learn

Materials:
- "Mr. Big Mouth" #1 (page 103)
- "Happy Tooth" and "Sudsy Tooth" (page 104)
- "Decayed Tooth" and "Mr. Plaque" (page 105)
- toothbrush

"Do you have teeth? Can you point to your teeth?" *(Point out your teeth. Introduce Mr. Big Mouth.)* "He has lots of shiny teeth." *(Take out the tooth with the smile on it.)* "His teeth are happy because he keeps them clean with his toothbrush." *(Hold up a toothbrush. Show "Happy Tooth" and "Sudsy Tooth.")* "Our teeth are happy when they are clean. This tooth is getting a sudsy toothpaste bath. Do you know why he needs a bath?" *(Introduce "Mr. Plaque.")* "He likes to sneak into our mouths every time we eat. Then he hides in our teeth and tries to chew holes in them. If we don't get him brushed out of our teeth, he makes our teeth look like this." *(Show "Decayed Tooth.")* "Oooo! That hurts!"

Demonstrate how to properly brush, using Mr. Big Mouth and the toothbrush. You should make little round circles over all of the teeth so that you get in every crack. Let each child have a turn brushing Mr. Big Mouth's teeth in the proper way. "Mr. Big Mouth wants you to learn how to keep your teeth clean and safe from Mr. Plaque."

■ Activities

BRUSH YOUR TEETH

Materials:
- toothbrush for each child
- toothpaste (optional)

Allow children to practice brushing their own teeth correctly. If there is not a sink available or your class size is rather large, you don't have to use toothpaste. The brushing technique works the same without it.

MR. BIG MOUTH (CRAFT)

Materials:

For each child:
- "Mr. Big Mouth" #2 (page 106)
- ten 1" x 3/4" white rectangles for teeth
- crayons
- glue
- wet sponge or rag for sticky fingers

Let children glue the teeth in Mr. Big Mouth's mouth. Let the projects be their own. The main objective of these projects is to develop small muscle coordination and have fun doing it.

■ Closing

Materials:

For each child:
- "Tooth Chart" (page 107)
- five star stickers

This chart is to be posted in the children's bathrooms or bedrooms to remind them to brush their teeth every day. Every time children brush their teeth during the week, they can put a star on the charts. Encourage children to share the information they learned today with family members at home. "Our teeth are happy when we give them a toothpaste shampoo, because that's how we get rid of mean old Mr. Plaque." Remember to ask children if they are using their charts at home.

Mr. Big Mouth #1

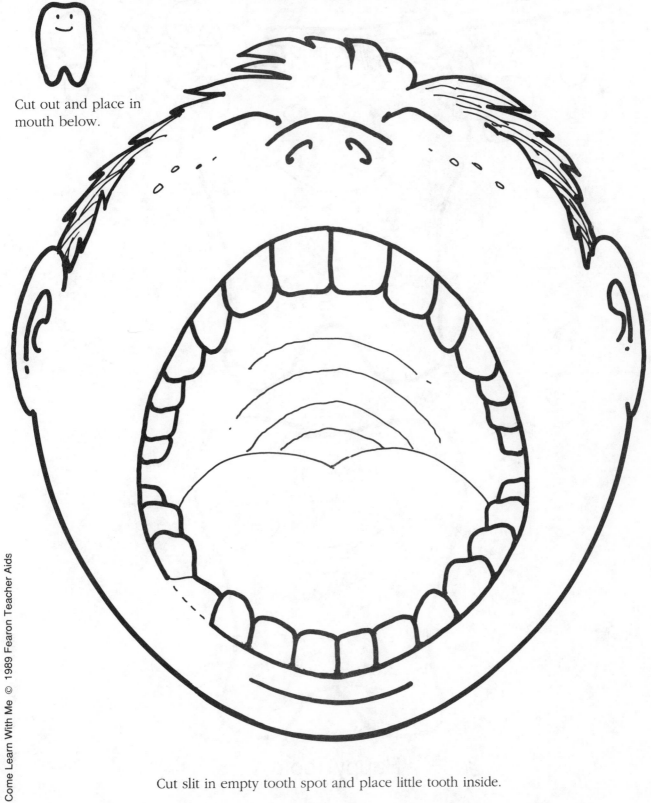

Cut out and place in mouth below.

Cut slit in empty tooth spot and place little tooth inside.

Learning to Brush Our Teeth

Sudsy Tooth

Happy Tooth

Decayed Tooth

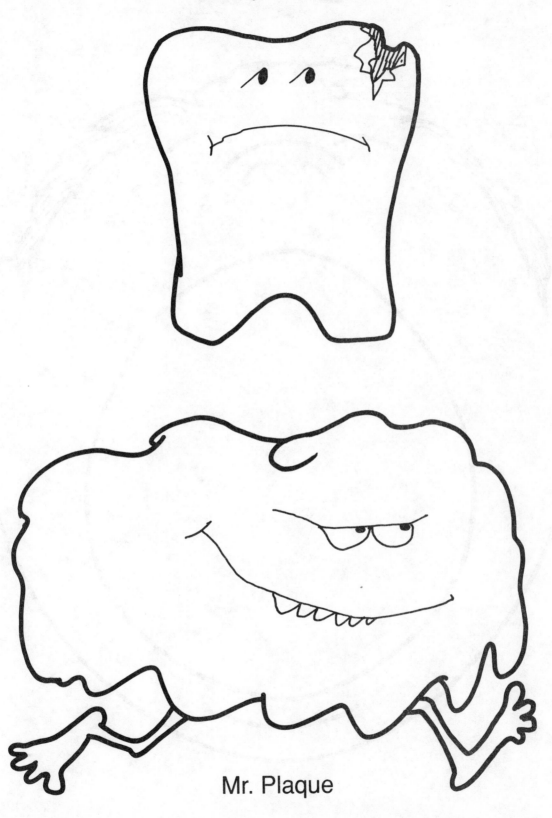

Mr. Plaque

Learning to Brush Our Teeth

Mr. Big Mouth #2

My Tooth Chart

Put a star under each day that you remember to brush your teeth.

Monday	Tuesday	Wednesday	Thursday	Friday

Happy and Sad Faces

Use with "Tooth Friends" project in next lesson.

Learning to Brush Our Teeth

More About Teeth

■ Opening Activities
(pages 38–39)

■ Listen and Learn
Materials:
- "Mr. Big Mouth" #1 (page 103)
- "Happy Tooth" and "Sudsy Tooth" (page 104)
- "Decayed Tooth" and "Mr. Plaque" (page 105)

Hold up the pictures of Mr. Plaque and the three teeth one at a time, and see if children remember the pictures. If not, just tell them and let them repeat after you. Pantomime with the children how to correctly brush teeth. Begin with unscrewing the cap on the toothpaste tube, and finish with rinsing out your mouth after a thorough job of brushing. Make sound effects of water running in the sink, etc. During the actual brushing, use the tune to "Here We Go Round the Mulberry Bush" and sing the following song:

This Is the Way!
This is the way we brush our teeth,
Brush our teeth, brush our teeth.
This is the way we brush our teeth,
So early in the morning.

Repeat several times.

■ Storytime
Materials:
- "I Don't Want Holes in My Teeth" or any short story about proper dental hygiene or a visit to the dentist's office

This story is about a little bunny who doesn't brush her teeth, and as a result, Mr. Plaque chews a hole in one of them. The bunny has to visit the dentist. Talk about experiences children may have had at the dentist. Point out fillings in your teeth or a child's tooth. "Listen carefully to the story, to find out what the bunny did wrong and why Mr. Plaque was able to chew a hole in one of her teeth." Read the story.

◼ Activities

TOOTH FRIENDS (CRAFT)
Materials:
For each child:
- "Tooth Friends" activity page (page 110)
- two happy and two sad faces (page 107)
- small piece of foil
- yellow crayon
- glue
- wet sponge or rag for sticky fingers

Have the faces already cut out for children and a demonstration set for yourself. Demonstrate how to make the "Tooth Friends" project as you tell the following story:

This first tooth is clean and white.*(Point to the first tooth.)* That's how our teeth start out. He is a happy tooth.*(Glue on a happy face.)* This is how our poor teeth will look if no one brushes them.*(Begin to color the second tooth yellow.)* They will get all yellow and gooey with plaque and food. No one ever brushes mean old Mr. Plaque off. That makes our teeth sad.*(Glue on a sad face and begin to color the third tooth yellow also.)* Mr. Plaque has been very busy. Can you see the hole he chewed in this tooth? Ooo! That hurts! When there is a hole in the tooth, you can't brush it away.*(Glue a sad face on the third tooth.)* You will have to go to the dentist. The dentist will clean off Mr. Plaque and fill the hole with silver.*(Glue the foil over the hole on the last tooth, and glue on a happy face.)* Now our tooth friend is clean and white again with just a little silver Band-Aid to cover the hole. We need to keep him brushed, so he will stay clean and safe from mean old Mr. Plaque.

Give children an opportunity to make the Tooth Friends. Remember that process, not product, is what is important. Associating the white teeth with healthy, happy teeth will benefit the children.

◼ Closing

Remind children that it is often easy to be lazy like Lacy, but to keep teeth healthy, regular brushing is important. Sing "This Is the Way We Brush Our Teeth" (page 108) again.

Tooth Friends

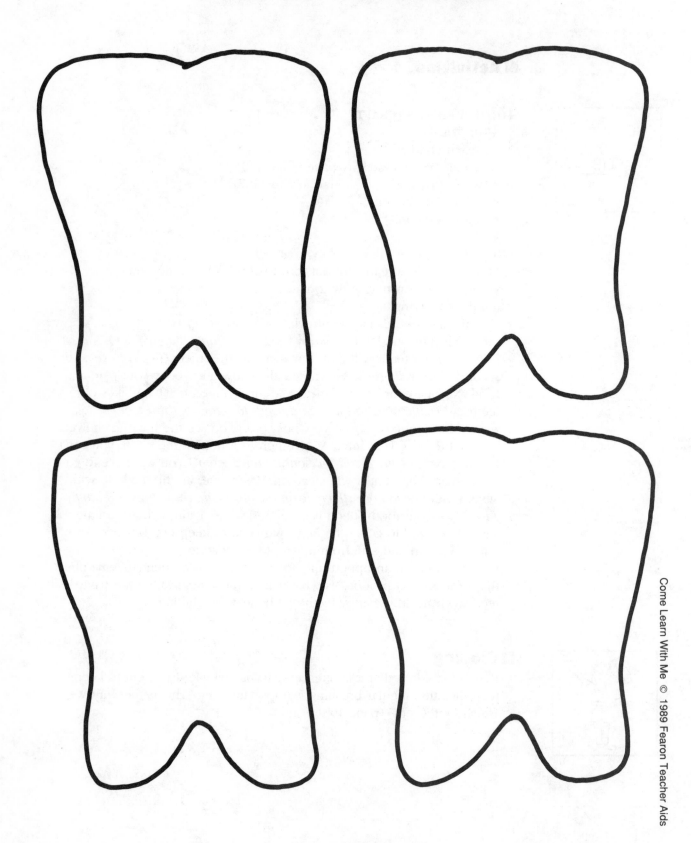

More About Teeth

Farm Animals

■ Opening Activities

(pages 38–39)

■ Listen and Learn

Materials:
- flannel board
- "Farm Animals" (colored and cut out, page 114)
- pig figure (page 115)

Introduce the pig fingerplay by asking children if they can make the sound a pig makes. If none of the children can make the sound, demonstrate it and ask the children to copy you. Compliment them for attempting to make any sounds.

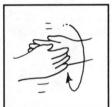

> Two mother pigs living in a pen,
> *(Hold both thumbs up and wiggle them.)*
> Each had four babies, that makes ten.
> *(Wiggle all ten fingers.)*
> Four little piggies were black and white.
> *(Wiggle four fingers.)*
> Four little piggies were black as night.
> *(Wiggle other four fingers.)*
> All eight piggies loved to play,
> *(Wiggle all your fingers.)*
> So they rolled and they rolled in the mud all day.
> *(Roll your hands.)*

Put flannel board animal figures up one at a time. Ask children to name them. Tell children the names of unrecognized animals, and let them repeat after you. Use your judgment according to the age and ability of the children to determine how many animals to put on the flannel board. After the animals are up, make an animal sound. Let a child come up to the board and choose the animal that makes that sound. Compliment the children for their efforts. Remember, this is not a test.

■ Storytime

Materials:
- "Breakfast on the Farm" or any short story about farm animals or products
- cow figure (page 116)

Ask children where milk comes from. Let them respond. Hold up the cow figure. Point out the udder, and explain how a cow is milked. Say, "Listen carefully to the story, and see how Sarah and her aunt, uncle, and cousins prepare for breakfast."

■ Activities

FEED THE ANIMALS (DRAMATIC PLAY)
"There are so many things to do on a farm. All of the animals need to be fed. Let's pretend we are on a farm and we are going to take care of the animals. Let's start with the chickens. Everybody get a bucket of wheat to feed the chickens. They like to eat their food right on the ground, so we need to spread the wheat on the ground for them like this." Make an underhand toss with your hand after pretending to get some wheat out of your bucket.

Sing "This Is the Way We Feed the Chickens" to the tune of "Here We Go Round the Mulberry Bush" while doing the pantomime. Try other verses and actions such as, "This is the the way we milk the cow . . . ," "This is the way we feed the horses . . . ," "This is the way we feed the pigs . . ." Allow children to make up other verses.

FARM SCENE (CRAFT)
Materials:
For each child:
- "On the Farm" activity page (page 117)
- animal stickers
- crayons (optional)

Allow children to stick the animals around the barn on their papers. The barn can also be colored. Discuss what is happening in the picture as the children work.

ANIMAL STICK PUPPETS (CRAFT)
Materials
- farmer figure (page 114) and popsicle stick
- glue

For each child:
- one "Farm Animal" figure (page 114)
- one popsicle stick
- crayons

Cut out and glue a farm animal figure on a popsicle stick for each child. Have children color the farm animals as you color the farmer. Sing the following song with the children:

Old MacDonald Had a Farm
Old MacDonald had a farm E-I-E-I-O
And on his farm he had a cow E-I-E-I-O
With a "moo, moo" here and a "moo, moo" there
Here a "moo," there a "moo"
Everywhere a "moo, moo."
Old MacDonald had a farm E-I-E-I-O.

Let children come up in front of the class with their animals one at a time. Sing a verse about each animal.

■ Closing

Do the pig fingerplay (page 111) once again. Make animal noises and ask children to name the animals. "The next time you drink a glass of milk, remember that we get milk from cows."

Farm Animals

Farm Animals

Pig

Farm Animals

Cow

Come Learn With Me © 1989 Fearon Teacher Aids

On the Farm

Baby Farm Animals

■ Opening Activities
(pages 38–39)

■ Listen and Learn
Materials:
- baby animal puppets mounted on popsicle sticks (page 120)
- farmer puppet on stick

Give children hints, and let them guess which animal you are describing: This animal is soft and white. It likes to eat grass with its mama. This animal says, "Baaa."*(lamb)*

This animal is small and pink. It has a curly tail and a round nose. This animal likes to sleep in the mud. This animal says "Oink, oink."*(pig)* This animal is smaller than a lamb or pig. It is soft and yellow. It has feathers. It can swim. It says, "Quack, quack."*(duckling)*

This animal is even smaller than a duck. It is soft, fluffy, and yellow. It says, "Peep, peep." It likes to eat little bugs and worms. Its mama lays eggs and says, "Cluck, cluck."*(chick)*

This animal is bigger than a chick or a duckling or a pig or a lamb. This animal likes to drink its mother's milk. It says, "Maa," and its mother says, "Moo."*(baby cow or calf)*

This baby animal is as big as a baby calf. It is soft and has long legs. When it grows big, this baby can give you rides on its back. It says, "Neigh."*(a baby horse or foal)*

Show the stick puppet after each animal has been guessed. Also allow children to imitate the animal sounds. If children are real young, shorten the hints by just asking what animal makes a particular sound. Sing "Old MacDonald Had a Farm" using the animal puppets. Let one child hold the farmer while standing beside you. Let another child pick an animal to hold as you sing about it.

■ Storytime
Materials:
- "Stay Close to Mother" or any short story about baby farm animals and the protection their mothers provide

This story is about Charley Chick who decides to venture out on his own after being warned not to. Besides pointing out that baby farm animals receive protection from their mothers, the story also teaches the importance of obedience. "Listen carefully to the story, and see what danger Charley Chick finds on the farm." Read the story.

■ Activities

WHERE IS MY MOTHER? (CRAFT)
Materials:
For each child:
- "Where Is My Mother?" activity page (page 121)
- baby animals (page 122)
- glue
- wet sponge or rag for sticky fingers

Instruct children to glue the baby animals next to the correct mothers. For younger children, learning to use glue is more the goal of the project than actually matching the pictures. As children get older, they will be more interested with matching.

WHAT'S MISSING? (GAME)
Materials:
- animal puppets used in the beginning of the lesson

Hold three animal puppets in your hand for children to see and name. Then put all three animals behind your back, and take one of them away. Bring the remaining two animals back so that children can see them again. Ask children to name the missing animal. Give praise even if you have to supply the answer. Continue with a different set of animals.

MAGNET FRIENDS (CRAFT)
Materials:
For each child:
- "Magnet Friends" (page 122)
- cotton ball
- one pink and one yellow pom-pom
- three magnet strips
- glue
- wet sponge or rag for sticky fingers

Have children glue cotton on the baby lamb, a yellow pom-pom on the baby chick, and a pink pom-pom on the baby pig. Glue magnet strips on the back of each one, and the baby animals can be used as refrigerator magnets.

■ Closing

Sing "Old MacDonald Had a Farm" or do a favorite fingerplay. Remind children of Charley Chick and the lesson he learned about obedience.

119

Baby Animal Puppets

Color, cut out, and glue on popsicle sticks.

Baby Farm Animals

Where Is My Mother?

Directions: Glue the baby animal next to its mother.

Baby Farm Animals

Baby Animals

(Cut out and use with "Where Is My Mother?" activity page.)

Magnet Friends

Cut out around circle and complete according to page 119.

Baby Farm Animals

Fish

■ Opening Activities
(pages 38–39)

■ Listen and Learn
Materials:
- "Fish Friends" (page 126)
- flannel board

"Do you know where fish live? Do they live in a house? Do they live in trees? Do they live in the water?" Put the five "Fish Friends" on the flannel board, and do the following fingerplay:

> Five little fish swam out to sea.
> This one said, "I'm as hungry as can be."
> *(Rub your stomach.)*
> This one said, "Here's a worm for me."
> *(Wiggle your finger.)*
> This one said, "Wait, we better look."
> This one said, "I see a hook."
> This one said, "We better swim away."
> *(Make a swimming motion with your arms, and continue through next line.)*
> So they swam and they swam and they swam far away.

Repeat several times.

■ Storytime

Materials:
- "Fish Belong in the Ocean and Little Boys Belong in a House" or any short story about fish and how their needs are different from ours.

This story is about a little boy named Shane who pretends to be living in the ocean with the fish while he is taking a bath. He soon realizes that the ocean is no place for a little boy to live. "Listen carefully to the story to find out some ways that fish are different from little boys." After the story comment about all the different kinds of fish in the ocean. Ask children questions that point out differences between people and fish: "Do you like to eat anchovies? Fish do. Do you think fish eat pizza?"

■ Activities

RING AROUND THE FISHIES (GAME)
Materials:
- "Fish Friends" from earlier in the lesson
- flannel board

Remind children how Shane played "Ring Around the Rosie" with an octopus in the story. Show the picture on that page again. Have children make a circle and hold hands. Put all five fish in the center of the circle. Sing the following song together:

> Ring around the fishies
> Pocketful of worms
> Ashes, ashes
> We all fall down!
> Repeat several times.

LET'S GO FISHING (DRAMATIC PLAY)
Materials:
- fishing pole for each child (Use a popsicle stick. Tie a string to one end, and attach a magnet for a hook on the other end. A glue gun works great for attaching the magnet to the string.)
- "Fish Friends" with paper clips attached to their mouths

Let each child have a turn catching fish. The magnet on the end of the fishing pole will attract the paper clip on the fish's mouths. If you don't have a fishing pole for each child, the poles can be shared. Give children some tips on how to catch fish: They can try sliding the magnet along the floor. Also, children must be sure to touch the magnet to the paper clip because that is the only part of the fish that will stick to the "hook."

MAKE A FISH (CRAFT)
Materials:
For each child:
- two fish (page 127)
- four plastic eyes
- two paper clips
- glue
- crayons
- wet sponge or rag for sticky fingers

Have children color both sides of their fish and glue on the eyes. When finished, attach paper clips to the fish's mouths, and add them to the pile of fish to "catch" with the fishing poles.

Row Your Boat (dramatic play)
Materials:
• fish from previous art project
Divide children into small groups of two or three. Have them sit on the floor facing each other in a straddle position to make a "boat." Have children spread the fish out around the "boat," hold hands, and sing the following song as they rock back and forth:

Row, Row, Row Your Boat
Row, row, row your boat
Gently out to sea.
Merrily, merrily, merrily, merrily
We'll catch some fish, you'll see!

Pretend to row out far enough to reach a good fishing spot while singing. "This looks like a great place to fish!" Allow children to catch the fish, using their poles. Then pretend to row home, while singing once again. Add some interesting comments on the journey home: "Oh! I think I see a shark! Let's get out of here." Then row and sing as fast as you can.

■ Closing
Choose a favorite fingerplay or review and discuss the pictures in today's story. Ask children to share real fishing trip experiences they may have had.

Fish Friends

1. I'm hungry as can be.

2. There's a worm for me.

3. Wait, we better look.

4. It's on a hook!

5. We better swim away.

Fish

Give each child two fish to color and glue plastic eyes on.

Fish

Birds

■ Opening Activities
(pages 38–39)

■ Listen and Learn

Materials:
- "Baby Birds" (page 132)
- "Bird's Nest" activity page (page 131)
- small sticks
- flannel board
- pieces of yarn
- glue

"Today we are going to talk about birds. Do you like birds? They are pretty to look at, and some of them sing pretty songs. There are blue birds, red ones, brown ones, and black birds. But one of the things I like best about birds is that they fly." Do the following fingerplay with the children:

The Little Bird
I saw a little birdie go hop, hop, hop.
(Use two fingers to hop across your arm.)
I told the little birdie to stop, stop, stop.
(Shake your finger in rhythm to the words, "Stop, stop, stop.")
I went to the window to say, "How do you do?"
But he spread his little wings and away he flew.
(Put your thumbs together and wave your hands like a bird flying away.)

Repeat several times. Sometimes children need specific instructions on how to move their hands for the fingerplay. Take a line at a time, and help the children get their fingers working.

Tape the "Bird's Nest" activity page to the flannel board. Have the yarn, sticks, and baby birds ready to glue on the paper as you talk about how birds build nests:

"Birds make their homes in the trees. They like to be way up high in the trees, so cats and dogs and little boys and girls can't reach them. Do you think bird houses look like our houses? No, they don't. The mother and father bird build a nest out of little sticks, grass, soft feathers, or anything else they can find." *(Glue sticks and yarn on the nest. Cup your hands together to show the approximate size of the nest.)* "When the nest is made, the mother bird lays some eggs in it. The mother or father bird sits on the eggs in the nest to keep them warm and safe for a long time.

Finally the baby birds are ready to come out. They use their little sharp beaks to peck out of their egg shells." *(Glue the baby birds in the nest.)* "Now we have two baby birds that are very hungry!"

■ Storytime

Materials:
- "Baby Jake, Get Up and Fly," or any short story about a baby bird's first flight

This story is about a baby bird who does not heed the warning of his parents to stay in his nest, and thinking he can fly, he falls out. "Listen carefully to find out what happens to Jake when he falls out of his nest." Read the story.

■ Activities

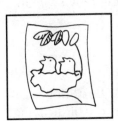

BIRD'S NEST (CRAFT)

Materials:

For each child:
- "Bird's Nest" activity page (page 131)
- "Baby Birds" (page 132)
- small pieces of yarn
- twigs or brown construction paper strips
- glue
- wet sponge or rag for sticky fingers

Have children make nests just as you demonstrated earlier in the lesson. Part of this activity could include going outside to gather sticks or twigs to use for the nests. After the nests are completed, children can glue the baby birds inside.

BIRDIE, BIRDIE (GAME)

Divide the children in half, and separate them on opposite sides of the room. Encourage children to flap their arms like birds and pretend to fly. "Oh, what good birds you are!" Demonstrate how the game begins by "flying" over to a child on the other side of the room and saying, "Birdie, Birdie, how's your neighbor?" The child will answer, "I don't know. I'll go ask." This child "flies" to the other side of the room and asks another child, "Birdie, Birdie, how's your neighbor?" That child repeats the same answer and flies to the other side to ask a neighbor. "Birdies" will be flying back and forth across the room for the entire game. Children may not be able to say the correct words, but they can flap their arms and fly across the room, even if you have to say the words.

FLYING BIRD (CRAFT)
Materials:
- stapler

For each child:
- "Bird Body" (page 132)
- popsicle stick
- 18" piece of yarn
- small feather
- glue
- crayons
- wet sponge or rag for sticky fingers

Before beginning, staple one end of the yarn to the bird. Tie the other end to the popsicle stick. Have children glue the feathers on the bird bodies for wings and draw eyes. Children can "fly" the birds by swinging them in the air.

■ Closing

Review what a bird uses to build a nest, or do "The Little Bird" fingerplay (page 128). "On your way home today, see if you notice any birds flying in the sky."

Bird's Nest

Bird Body

Trace and cut out of red, blue, or brown construction paper.

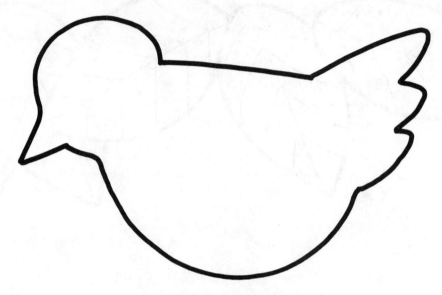

bird pattern
1 per child

- -

Baby Birds

Birds

Jungle Animals

■ Opening Activities
(pages 38–39)

■ Listen and Learn
Materials:
- animal visual aids from past lessons
- flannel board
- assembled "Elephant" (page 137)

Ask children to name any of the animals talked about in previous lessons. Put animal figures on the flannel board as children name them. Hold up the pictures of unmentioned animals, and ask children to name them. If children are unable to name an animal, provide the name. Then let children repeat after you. It takes time and repetition for little ones to learn the names of animals. Praise them for any efforts made in response to your questions. Discuss where these animals live, and tell children that this lesson will be about animals that live in the jungle. Ask children to think of a very big animal, and then put the elephant up on the flannel board. See if anyone can name this animal. Look around the room, and compare the size of an elephant to something children can see. "The elephant is the biggest four-footed animal on land today. He has a long nose. His nose is called a trunk. He doesn't have hands like us, so he uses his trunk to pick up things. The elephant can pick up big trees with his strong trunk. He can even pick up you! He can also pick up very small things like a peanut. Do you know what he does when he wants to take a bath? He fills his trunk with water, then he puts it over his head and sprays the water all over himself. It's just like taking a shower. Doesn't the elephant have a wonderful nose?"

■ Storytime
Materials:
- "Where Is My Baby?" or any short story about jungle animals

This story is about a mother elephant who loses her baby. In the process of looking for her baby, she finds many other kinds of jungle animal babies. "Listen carefully to the story, and look at the pictures to see what other jungle animals you might see." Read the story.

■ Activities

CAN YOU MATCH? (GAME)
Materials:
- flannel board
- "Jungle Animals" (page 136)
- "Where Is My Baby?" story

Put up all the jungle animals on the flannel board. You may find that using only two or three animals at a time works best for your group of children. Then open the "Where Is My Baby?" story to a page with an animal pictured on it. Ask children to find and name the same animal on the flannel board. You may need to hold the flannel board figures side by side with the book before children can see which animal matches.

ELEPHANT (CRAFT)
Materials:
For each child:
- "Elephant" (page 137)
- brad fastener
- glue
- wet sponge or rag for sticky fingers

As children glue the ears on their elephants, talk about features that make an elephant unique. Besides having a long nose, the elephant has big ears. He can use his ears to fan himself. Ask children if they can wiggle their ears. Attach the elephant's trunk with a brad so that it will be movable.

Do the following action rhyme with the children:

I'm a big elephant, stomping through the jungle.
(Lean over and clasp hands together for your trunk. Swing your "trunk" back and forth, and lift your feet as if stomping through the jungle.)
Now I am a little mouse sneaking so quietly.
(Stoop down and sneak quietly.)
Big things,
(Hold hands up high.)
Little things,
(Hold hands down low.)
Everywhere I see.
(Hold hands above eyes and look back and forth.)

Little mouse,
(Stoop down for mouse.)
Or elephant,
(Stand up in elephant position.)
Which one will it be?

Give children practice determining which is big and which is little. Stoop down low like a mouse, or stand up tall like an elephant, and have children identify "big" or "little." Have a child do the stooping or standing for the other children to guess. You may need to whisper suggestions in the child's ear: "Why don't you try being a mouse? Do you need to be big or little?" Give hints as necessary. This is a learning experience.

GIRAFFE (CRAFT)
Materials:
- "Giraffe" for each child (page 138)
- small sponge pieces
- yellow and black paint in shallow trays
- paint shirts

Children can use a large shirt buttoned on backward for a paint shirt. Show children the giraffe in the "Where Is My Baby?" story and have them notice the spots. Have them look at their giraffe pictures. See if children notice there are no spots on the pictures. Have them dip sponge pieces into the paint and make sponge print spots on the giraffes.

■Closing
Review ways an elephant can use his trunk, or repeat the elephant fingerplay. Ask children if they have ever been to the zoo and have seen any of these jungle animals.

Jungle Animals

Jungle Animals

Elephant

Reproduce on gray construction paper and cut out for each child.

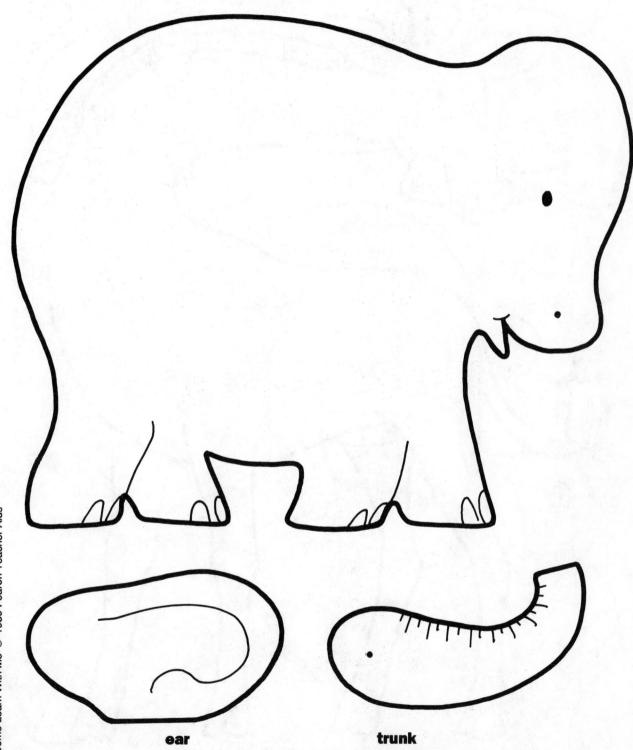

ear

trunk

Jungle Animals

Giraffe

Jungle Animals

Circles

■ Opening Activities

(pages 38–39)

■ Listen and Learn

Materials:
- "Sally Circle" stick puppet (page 142)
- "See My Circle" picture (page 143)
- "Train" picture (page 144)

Introduce Sally Circle. Explain that a circle is round and that there are circles everywhere. Show children the "Train" and "See My Circle" pictures, and ask them to point out the circles. If children cannot see the circles, point them out. Hold Sally Circle next to the circles, so they can compare the shapes. Have children make a little circle with both hands, and then begin the following fingerplay:

> Here's a little ball,
> And a bigger ball,
> *(Make the ball larger . . .)*
> And a great big ball I see.
> *(. . . and larger.)*
> Are you ready, shall we count them?
> One, two, three.
> *(Repeat the three ball sizes with your hands.)*

Repeat several times.

■ Storytime

Materials:
- "Bubbles" or any short story about shapes (especially circles)

This story is about a little girl named Judy who decides to take a bubble bath. She puts too much bubble bath in the tub and ends up having a huge mess to clean up. The pictures give children many opportunities to see circle-shaped bubbles, and the story also teaches a lesson of responsibility. "As you listen to the story, look closely at the pictures, and see how many circles you can find." Read the story.

■ Activities

MAKING BUBBLES
Materials:
- milk (powdered works well!)
- cup and straw for each child

Pour milk into each child's cup, and let children use straws to blow bubbles. You may want to set a limit of blowing bubbles only to the top of the cup and not letting them overflow. Have children watch the bubbles pop before more are blown. Point out that bubbles are circles.

WHEELS ON A TRAIN (CRAFT)
Materials:
For each child:
- "Train" activity page (page 144)
- six 1" and two 1 1/2" construction paper circles
- glue
- crayons
- wet sponge or rag for sticky fingers

Have children glue the train wheels on the appropriate-size wheels on their papers. For very young children, gluing the circles anywhere on the paper is an accomplishment. It is better not to "fix" a child's picture so that it is "right." It is not always easy to decide how much help to give a child, but keep in mind that young children like to do things themselves.

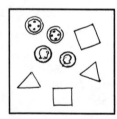

MAKE A PILE (SORTING)
Materials:
- buttons, pennies, squares, triangles, and other shapes

Mix all the shapes together, and have children sort them in various ways. They can begin by finding all the circles, and then sorting all the shapes into piles. Children can also count the circles. Muffin tins make versatile sorting containers. Vary the activity according to the success of the children. Remember, they enjoy repetition also.

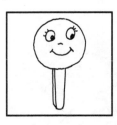

WHERE'S SALLY? (GAME)

Materials:
- "Sally Circle" stick puppet for each child (page 142)
- a collection of construction paper shapes in various sizes (circles, squares, rectangles, triangles)

Give each child a Sally Circle stick puppet. Hold up a construction paper shape, and ask children to hold up "Sally" if the shape is a circle. Repeat with different shapes.

■ Closing

Do a favorite fingerplay. Play a circle game. Point out circles in the classroom, or give children ideas of where to find circles at home (dinner plate, clocks, wheels on a car, rim of a glass).

Sally Circle Stick Puppets

Cut out "Sally" and glue on
a popsicle stick.

See My Circle

Circles

Train

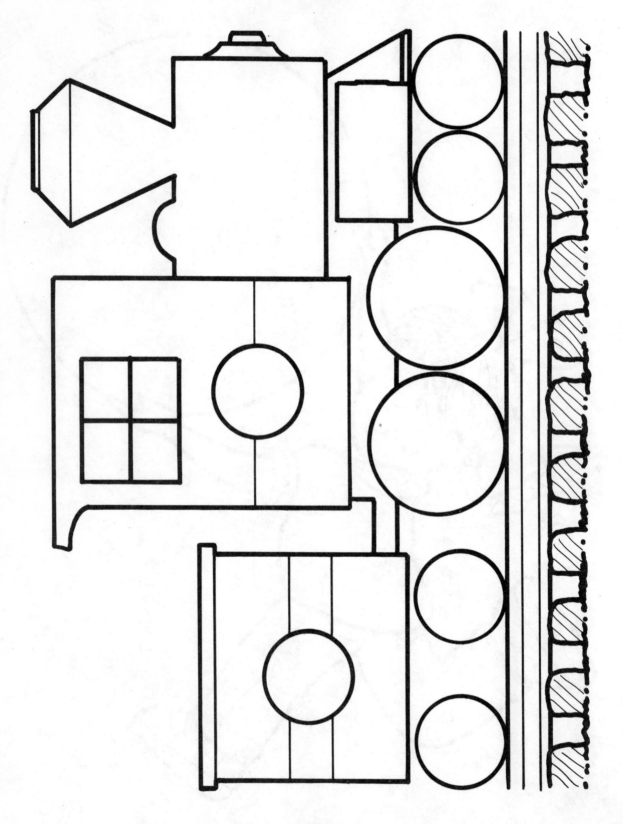

Circles